TELLING STORIES

Library of Congress Cataloging-in-Publication Data
Names: Martin, Lee, 1955– author.
Title: Telling stories: the craft of narrative and the
writing life / Lee Martin.
Description: Lincoln: University of Nebraska Press, 2017.
Identifiers: LCCN 2017013385 (print)
LCCN 2017029103 (ebook)
ISBN 9781496202932 (epub)
ISBN 9781496202949 (mobi)
ISBN 9781496202956 (pdf)
ISBN 9781496202024 (paperback: alk. paper)
ISBN 1496202023 (paperback: alk. paper)
Subjects: LCSH: Authorship. | Creative writing. | Nar-
ration (Rhetoric) | Storytelling. | BISAC: LANGUAGE
ARTS & DISCIPLINES / Composition & Creative Writ-
ing. | LANGUAGE ARTS & DISCIPLINES / Authorship.
Classification: LCC PN145 (ebook) | LCC PN145 .M38
2017 (print) | DDC 808.02—dc23
LC record available at
https://lccn.loc.gov/2017013385

Set in ITC New Baskerville by Rachel Gould.

For Cathy, who understands when
I go away to play with words

CONTENTS

ACKNOWLEDGMENTS

My fourth grade teacher once told me I had no imagination. I've never forgotten. This is a book for all those who dare to dream and to devote themselves to the craft of writing. My lifelong apprenticeship started when I first fell in love with the power of story. Along the way I've had the privilege of learning from those more advanced than I and passing on what I've learned to others. I've been blessed with a teaching career that now approaches its thirty-sixth year. I'm so grateful for everyone I've met along my journey. To try to name you all would be a fool's game. If I sat in your classroom or you in mine—if we had the chance to talk about writing, wherever we might have been—you had a part in this book. For that I thank you, and I wish you a happy life, rich with the stories you have to tell. I'm so blessed to be a part of this family of writers. May we all keep doing the good work. Peace and love.

them that create the most memorable characters in works of fiction and nonfiction. If we give our characters free will—if we don't fully know them too soon—they can take us to some interesting places that can either illuminate or complicate, or do both things at once, the thrust of our exploration of any particular subject. Our characters have to be able to surprise us, and the plot of a good story usually puts enough pressure on them until they can't help but reveal who they really are. "The personal life of every individual is based on secrecy," Chekhov writes in "The Lady with the Pet Dog." A good story doesn't allow that secrecy to stand. A good story strips it away and leaves the character, to borrow from Woody Allen, "without feathers."

The Art of the Detail

A combination of sensory details can fully immerse readers in a scene and establish a writer's authority. Readers are more willing to trust and follow a writer when they feel that the writer has a great deal of confidence in what he or she is portraying on the page. Scenes need to happen in specific locales; otherwise, they can seem not to have happened at all. Sensory details are the tools of the trade that the writer uses to convince us that something really happened. A carefully chosen detail can also provide an indirect path toward what the writer has come to say. Don't say, "I'm going to write a story of the loss of faith." Instead, à la Flannery O'Connor in "Good Country People," say: "I'm going to write about a woman with a wooden leg. I'm going to see where that leg might take me."

The Art of Point of View

A good story locates itself within a particular consciousness. The interior journey of a point of view character provides an arc that coexists with the arc of the narrative. Readers want not only know to what happened but to also know the person who lived through the experience. It's the combination of the two that lends the narrative its significance.

The Art of Language

Mavis Gallant, in her brief essay about style in writing, says, "The only question worth asking about a story—or a poem, or a piece of sculpture, or a new concert hall—is, 'Is it dead or alive?'" A piece breathes life in part from the style in which the writer has chosen to bring it to the page. As Gallant goes on to point out, "If a work of the imagination needs to be coaxed into life, it is better scrapped and forgotten." Style, she says, should never be separate from structure, which I take to mean the manner of telling should always be in the service of what's being told. Put another way, style is part of the form, and the form and the content and the meaning must be part of the same whole in order for the writer to say what he or she has come to the page to say. Style has always seemed like an instinctual matter to me. A voice emanating from the world of the work, a world the writer knows so well that he or she can't help but speak its language. It's amazing how an intimate knowledge of that world can make all sorts of decisions for a writer. Know your worlds, and everything falls into place, including the style of the writing. Prose writers, don't think that language is only the domain of the poets. Pay attention to sentence variety, word choice, prose rhythm, the sounds of words, metaphor, pacing, and the next thing you know, you'll be stylin'!

We tell stories because narrative allows us to make the lived life vivid to the readers, thereby convincing them that they share in the human experience being portrayed. We tell stories as a way of thinking through dramatization. From biblical parables through Aesop's fables to Grimm's fairy tales and beyond, people have hungered for narrative, not only as entertainment or a record of events but also because it is through story that we often explore what we don't know and find what we didn't know we were seeking. A teacher of mine used to say that a good short story led to a moment of surprise, which he defined as "more truth than we think we have a right to expect." The same holds true for a good piece of nonfiction. As we read, we participate in the writer's attempt to find what he or she didn't know when first coming to the page. Narrative is the art of constructing visual images, scenes if you will, that make a dreamworld for the readers and that require those readers' participation in the intellectual and emotional life of the story. A good story, then, dramatizes, explores, illuminates. Characters move through time and space and are profoundly changed because of the journey.

What follows is a journey through the various techniques of narrative. I hope the trip will be fruitful for both those who call themselves fiction writers and those who are interested in writing memoirs. Along the way I'll throw in some thoughts about the writing life with the hope of offering advice, encouragement, and inspiration.

We all have stories to tell. Let's get started.

TELLING STORIES

PART 1 ❧ Structure

Once upon a Time

"The king died and then the queen died"
is a story. "The king died, and then the
queen died of grief" is a plot.

—E. M. FORSTER

Writing the Opening of a Short Story

I wasn't sure I'd be able to run this morning. A light snow was falling, and the streets already had patches of ice on them from yesterday's storm. I walked a ways and had just about decided to play it safe. Then I saw a stretch of pavement with no ice on it, and I thought that maybe it wouldn't hurt to try to run a few steps. An hour later I stopped running.

Getting a new piece of writing started can be like that for me, as can picking up in the midst of a rough draft on a new writing day. I'm always a little fearful that I won't be up to the task, that I'll end up falling on my face, but I'm also stubborn. I like to keep moving forward. So, eventually, I begin. Maybe I write a sentence. Maybe I change a word or two in a sentence I've already written. The important thing is to make a move that engages me with the draft. I enter the stream of composition; the hours go by, and when I finally stop, I'm surprised by the number of words I've put on the page.

I've been working on a new short story lately, so after a good while spent writing the draft of a novel, I'm reacquainting myself with the way a story moves.

Which brings me to the starting out, those first steps the writer of the story makes onto the page, when he or she is trying to clearly state the givens of the premise while also getting the narrative moving forward. Raymond Carver described the early stages of his writing process as a matter of getting the bare bones on the page. "With the first draft," he said, "it's a question of getting down the outline, the scaffolding of the story. Then on subsequent revisions I'll see to the rest of it." Consider the opening of Carver's "Cathedral":

This blind man, an old friend of my wife's, he was on his way to spend the night. His wife had died. So he was visiting the dead wife's relatives in Connecticut. He called my wife from his in-laws'. Arrangements were made. He would come by train, a five-hour trip, and my wife would meet him at the station. She hadn't seen him since she worked for him one summer in Seattle years ago, but she and the blind man had kept in touch. They made tapes and mailed them back and forth. I wasn't enthusiastic about his visit. He was no one I knew. And his being blind bothered me. My idea of blindness came from the movies. In the movies, the blind moved slowly and never laughed. Sometimes they were led by seeing-eye dogs. A blind man in my house was not something I looked forward to.

So, what do we know about the world of the story? We know that a blind man, a former employer of the narrator's wife, is coming to spend the night. We know the blind man's wife has died, and we know how the narrator feels about that. Because of his faulty assumptions about blind people, he doesn't look forward to the visit. Notice how clearly and gracefully Carver gives us everything we need to know as we enter the world of the story. Things are in motion from the opening line, and a tension between the narrator and the blind man has been established before the guest arrives. Everything that the story needs to dramatize has been articulated.

A good story starts with a first step: *This blind man, an old friend of my wife's, he was on his way to spend the night.* Write a line that's already moving forward, that contains the story's premise. Then establish the perspective of the main character so we know his or her initial position when it comes to the premise: *A blind man in my house was not something I looked forward to.* Now you're ready to run. You're ready to follow the trail. Keep your eye out for those patches of ice, the ones that will cause the main character to slip and his or her initial position to shift. Do that, and you'll be like the narrator of "Cathedral," who at the end of the story is trying to draw a cathedral with the blind man's hand on top of his so the man can try to understand what such a building looks like. Like the narrator of Carver's story, you'll be amazed at where you've arrived: *It was like nothing else in my life up to now.* That's what a good story can do for us if we aren't afraid to set out. The journey can take us somewhere we didn't know we were going.

Juggling Balls

An Exercise for Opening a Short Story

For whatever reason I'm thinking this morning about the openings of short stories and what we expect of them. Rust Hills, in his excellent book *Writing in General and the Short Story in Particular*, says the end of a good story is always present in its beginning. The final move of a story is only possible because of everything set in motion in the opening.

For that reason I'm interested in stories that open with some degree of forward momentum. That momentum can come on a plot level from a sense of mystery or a problem to be solved, but it can also come more quietly, but just as urgently, from a character struggling with something. Maybe it's something about the self, or maybe it's something about a certain situation or another character in the story. Whatever it is, there's something to be resolved, and the story, from its opening words, is moving toward that resolution, or the lack of one, and all that it will mean to the characters involved. No matter how quiet the opening of a story may be, there's tension and urgency because stories are about characters moving through pivotal moments of their lives.

So, here's an exercise for opening a short story.

1. Open a story with a line something like this: "I was cutting wheat when Burton Quick came to tell me [fill in the rest of the line however you'd like.]" Something in this first line signals that the story is opening in the midst of something that will make this day unlike any other in our narrator's life.

2. Write a second line something like this: "At the house my

wife was [fill in the rest of the line however you'd like.]"
Often one story line isn't enough. Two elements of the
plot need to vibrate against each other to create a resonance. I assume from our opening two lines that whatever Burton Quick has come to say will bear upon whatever is at issue for the narrator and his wife.

3. Write a third line that contains the narrator's initial
   response to whatever his wife is doing at the house—
   something like this: "I'd told her [fill in the line however you'd like], but she wouldn't listen, so I'd decided to
   [again, fill this in however you'd like.]"

We now have three things to pay attention to in the story: (1)
whatever it is that Burton Quick has come to tell the narrator,
(2) whatever it is that the wife is doing in spite of her husband's
protestation, and (3) whatever the narrator thinks he's decided
to do. Three balls up in the air within three sentences. Quite
enough to arouse our curiosity, to make us keep writing to see
where things might go.

THE BONUS ROUND: Write a few lines that you imagine might
serve as a closing move. You're free to create whatever you'd
like, but I'll offer up a few lines as an example. "That's when my
wife surprised me by [fill it in]. It was like nothing I'd ever seen.
Burton Quick's story seemed like [fill it in]. I felt myself moving
toward something, and I [fill it in]."

The final move of the story, of course, may change as you write
the draft, but at least writing one now will give you some sense of
the sort of ending that you've made possible with your beginning.

Using Mystery to Open Your Story

Once in an undergraduate fiction workshop that I was teaching, I found myself talking about the value of mystery in the opening of a short story. Of course, there are a number of ways to open a story, but let's say you're desperate for one. Let's say you're in the prewriting stage of a new story, and not only are you at a loss for where to begin; you also have no knowledge of the characters or the plot. A good opening line that contains a bit of mystery may be just what you need.

Consider the following examples of first sentences:

> *I was in bed when I heard the gate.* (From Raymond Carver's "I Could See the Smallest Things")
> *I wake up afraid.* (From Tobias Wolff's "Next Door")
> *This is a story about an old lady who ordered a young man from an L.L. Bean catalog.* (From Ellen Gilchrist's "The Young Man")
> *On the platform at Penn Station, at 6:30 on a Saturday morning, a young woman in a red sweater stood waiting for the Boston train to pull in.* (From Joan Wickersham's "Commuter Marriage")

If you're like me, your curiosity is aroused by these openings. Questions arise from each sentence; there are things we want and need to know. Who's at the gate, and what will the narrator do next? Why does the narrator in the Wolff story wake up afraid? Afraid of what? Why would an old lady order a young man from L.L. Bean? How would that even be possible? What would happen if a young man actually arrived? Why is the young woman waiting for the train from Boston? Who's on that train, and what does he or she mean to the woman?

Imagine that you're the writer of each of these stories. How can you not keep writing from these opening sentences that give you so much to figure out? All you have to do is get your main characters into action. Maybe you'll see a causal chain of events begin to come together as your main characters respond to the mysteries that open their stories. If this happens, then this might happen, and so on, all the way to the end of the narrative.

To get the first draft of a story written, sometimes all you need is an opening line that has a bit of mystery in it. Often a story moves ahead from what the writer doesn't know. Norman Mailer once said, "Writer's block is only a failure of the ego." So, instead of fearing the blank page, march boldly onto it. Give yourself some questions to answer and keep writing until you have them. Open with a line that makes you curious, and then draft the story that eventually satisfies that curiosity. Start with what you don't know and end with what you do.

Trouble? I've Seen Trouble

I recently posted a quote from E. B. White on my Facebook group page, a quote that spoke to me about the importance of trouble when it comes to generating a plot: "There's no limit to how complicated things can get, on account of one thing always leading to another."

I've always agreed with those who say that creating a plot is a simple matter of getting a character into trouble and then seeing what he or she will do to try to get out of it. John Updike described his first steps onto the page in this way: "I try instantly to set in motion a certain forward tilt of suspense or curiosity, and at the end of the story or novel to rectify the tilt, to complete the motion." With that in mind I'd like to offer up a few ways to get your characters into trouble.

1. Sometimes trouble pays a visit. In Raymond Carver's "A Small, Good Thing" a young boy, Scotty, gets hit by a car, and though he appears to be unhurt at first, he later slips into a coma and then dies. His mother forgets about the cake that she ordered for his birthday from a baker who was abrupt with her. When the baker starts calling the house to say the cake hasn't been picked up—saying things like "Have you forgotten about Scotty?"—the trouble that started the story takes on an added dimension. No longer is it merely bad fortune striking. It's now something that requires a response, and that response is the eventual confrontation with the baker, which leads to a surprising moment of grace. The combination of bad luck and the presence of the baker leads us into the complicated terrain of suffering and compassion. If trouble puts pressure on a character, increase the pressure from a source outside the realm of the trouble. Press harder until your character has to act.

2. Sometimes we make our own trouble by what we decide to do. Sammy, the teenaged narrator of John Updike's "A&P," quits his job as a grocery clerk cashier in support of the girls who have violated decorum and come into the store in their bathing suits. Of course, his gesture goes unnoticed by the girls, and Sammy ends up with a consequence he couldn't have predicted: "My stomach fell as I felt how hard the world was going to be to me hereafter." Use dramatic irony to complicate the trouble-causing action. Let the character's intention produce its opposite result.

3. Sometimes we make our trouble by letting people believe something is true when it isn't. The central action of Ian McEwan's novel *Atonement* depends on thirteen-year-old Briony Tallis, who makes a false accusation based upon facts she believes to be true. Her accusation changes lives forever. There are variations of this plot-making strategy. Perhaps the character tells the truth about something heard or seen but leaves out other facts in order to let the listener construct the narrative that the speaker desires, a narrative that the speaker knows to be a partial truth. Sometimes a character says or does something only to have it misinterpreted. The key here is to arrange the facts in such a way, with whatever backstory is necessary, so more than one narrative is plausible.

4. Sometimes we make our trouble by trying to run away from what we've done or by being afraid of what we might do. The mathematics tutor Henry Dees in my novel *The Bright Forever* gives his pupil Katie Mackey a fatherly kiss on the cheek, but because he knows people already consider him an odd bird, he fears that if anyone were to have witnessed the kiss, they would consider him suspect. Adding to his fear is the fact that he's already started to question his own motivations. His fear leads him to a moment of paralysis at the time when he most needs to act, thereby creating a trouble that will haunt him the rest of his life. An entire plot can be spun from a character's questioning of his or her own action.

I'm particularly interested in how people create their own

troubles, either from the get-go or from how they respond to misfortunes that befall them. As the quote from E. B. White indicates, things will always get complicated if we let one thing follow another. If we can add a little pressure, irony, misinterpretation, or multilayered motivations, we can help those complications along. Too much restraint or politeness ruins a good narrative. Put your characters into action. Let them run at cross-purposes with others, with dramatic situations, and with themselves, and you'll create a memorable chain of events. We have to make room for the human flaws that can lead to trouble. Then we have to make enough room for our characters' attempts to save themselves. One thing leads to another. It's a good thing for a narrative to remember.

Making a Scene

When I was a boy, my mother often said to me, "Don't make a scene." Maybe I grew up to be a writer so I could make all the scenes I wanted. When we write narratives, whether fictional or the personal narratives of memoirs and essays, we need to give ourselves permission to make a scene.

I once had the pleasure of teaching a memoir writing workshop at the Warren County Public Library in Bowling Green, Kentucky. During the workshop we used objects from childhood (shoes, toys, scents) to recall pivotal moments from our pasts. Then we crafted scenes that invited the reader into the writer's memory and focused upon a moment of emotional resonance and complexity.

When people shared what they'd written, I heard stories of envy, desire, joy, disastrous circumstances—human moments, all of them shaped and delivered in a way that made me feel, and feel deeply, what the writers had felt when they lived through those moments.

Here are some reminders for writers of personal narratives:

1. Make sure that you've chosen an episode that was somehow outside the regular come and go of an ordinary day, an episode that includes a climactic moment beyond which life was never quite the same.
2. Set the scene right away in space and time and give us a sense of what the main characters carried with them into the scene. That emotional baggage plays a huge part in the characters' actions and reactions.
3. Include enough sensory detail to draw your reader into the scene. Remember that memoir isn't only a record of

what happened. It's a chance to put your readers into your shoes. A scene is built from small details. Don't neglect them.

4. Use the reflective voice of the writer at the desk to flesh out the complicated layers of the scene and how they played a role in shaping that writer's life. Remember that you're always a participant in the scene (the you of a younger age), but you're also the narrator looking back and making meaning from what happened.

5. Use dialogue and action to move the scene to its climax. This is all part of making the readers feel that they're with you in that moment.

Virginia Woolf said it isn't the thing that happened that matters the most but what the writer is able to make of the thing that happened. So, make a scene and see where it takes you in your thinking about how you came to be who you are in the here and now. Make a scene so your readers can participate in it. Step back from the scene, providing a voice-over as such, as you speak from the adult perspective, the person who is capable of knowing now what you didn't know then.

The Inevitable Surprise

Lately I've been thinking quite a bit about how a story gets resonance from the proper pairing of characters and the pressure of plot that causes something surprising and yet inevitable to rise at the end. As we all know, it's one thing to say this is what has to happen in order for a story to be memorable, and it's another thing to offer advice on how a writer makes this happen. With that in mind I'd like to consider Richard Bausch's story "The Fireman's Wife." I'd like to use this story to illustrate the techniques by which a short story writer leads us to the inevitable in a way that surprises us. Only in retrospect do we take note of what Bausch had to do in order to make his ending resonant and memorable, to make us believe we were reading one story when really we were reading another.

The opening of "The Fireman's Wife" immediately poses the question that drives the story: Will Jane leave her marriage to Martin? I like having a question to hang onto as we move through a story, something to be resolved by the end, rather than feeling as if we're moving through a series of scenes that seem to have been randomly selected. Everything from the opening of the story needs to be leaning toward what will eventually be the end. The key for the writer is to make that ending present from the get-go without the reader being overly aware of it, to let it rise covertly through the progression of the narrative.

The opening scene of "The Fireman's Wife" dramatizes an evening, growing long in the tooth, on which a group of friends have gathered. The men in the group aren't willing to let the night end. They may play cards. They may play the time-consuming game of Risk. Jane, though, has had enough of it all—enough of the evening, enough of the group, enough of her husband,

Martin: "She hasn't been married even two years and she feels crowded; she's depressed and tired every day. She never has enough time to herself. And yet when she's alone, she feels weak and afraid." Here's a woman leaning toward the door if she can only work up the courage to make the move. Toward the end of the opening scene, her friend Milly tells her that even she used to wonder whether she'd made a mistake in marrying her husband, Teddy. Then she says: "But, you know, all I had to do was wait. Just you know, wait for love to come around and surprise me again." Although we don't know it at the time, that line contains the story's end. The question becomes one of how Bausch keeps the end in doubt while moving toward it all along.

As Jane's dissatisfaction with her marriage deepens, another story takes shape, floating just below the primary narrative and for the most part out of sight. From time to time we glimpse it, and we may not even be sure of what we're seeing. At one point Jane surprises herself by telling a coworker that she thinks she'd like to have a baby. As one of my students smartly pointed out when we talked about this story, Jane seems to be trying on various lives for herself by latching onto the lives of those around her (her friend Milly is pregnant). At another point Jane views herself through the lens of her coworker's parents and the furnishings of their house: "Everything seems to stand for the kind of life she wants for herself: an attentive, loving husband, children; and a quiet house with a clock that chimes. She knows this is all very dreamy and childish, and yet she looks at Eveline's parents, those people with their almost thirty years' love, and her heart aches."

Passages such as these create that shadow narrative, the one that's rising. Add to these moments the one in which Jane, hearing the fire sirens, remembers what it was like when she and Martin were first married and she'd hear the sirens and worry about what might happen to him while out on a call. Jane has a longing for love and happiness, even a memory of tenderness, at the same time that she has a strong desire to leave the marriage.

Now notice how Bausch, just as this more tender story is working its way through the primary narrative of a marriage dissolving, pushes it back down a tad. The result is to thwart any certainty that we may think we have of where the story is headed. Jane thinks about all the Sundays she's spent in her in-laws' home, where her father-in-law's conversation is banal: "Jane realizes that she can't stand another Sunday afternoon listening to him talk. It comes to her like a chilly premonition, and quite suddenly, with a kind of tidal shifting inside her, she feels the full weight of her unhappiness." This move brings the primary narrative into sharp focus again and serves the purpose of inviting us to forget the more tender story of which we've had glimpses. It's at this point that Jane actually begins packing her bags in preparation for leaving Martin.

But before she can leave, Martin's fellow firefighters bring him home, his hands badly burned while fighting a fire. He sees the packed bags, and he knows what they mean even though Jane claims she just had too much to drink and was only going through what she has to wear. The next morning, while Martin sleeps, she goes outside and walks to the end of the driveway. There she takes in the neighborhood, the flatness of the Illinois plains, the clear day. She remembers what it felt like when they first moved into the neighborhood, and the particulars make clear it was a calm, hopeful feeling. She goes into the garage and sees Martin's model airplane engines. She remembers all the things that she liked best about him when they first met and fell in love. That tender story is rising again, and again Bausch pushes it back down: "She puts the engine down, thinking how people change. She knows she's going to leave him, but just for this moment, standing among these things she feels almost peaceful about it. She has, after all, no need to hurry. And as she steps out onto the lawn, she realizes that she can take her time to think clearly about when and where; she can even change her mind. But she doesn't think she will." The question posed in the opening of the story of whether Jane will leave her marriage seems to be answered, but wait, we have that shadow story, the more tender one, still in place. All it takes is the right arrangement of circumstances to make it rise above the primary story of a marriage ending.

An accident, a husband lying down to rest, a wife convinced that one day she'll leave him. They have a brief conversation. "Jane?" he says, and that one-word question is loaded with meaning. The subtext is clear. Will you forgive my shortcomings? Will you stay? Will you let us have another chance? She says: "Try to rest some more. You need to rest now." She can't give him the answer he wants, so she gives him no answer at all. She waits until he's asleep, and then she leaves the bedroom, closing the door. It's here, in the final paragraph, that the shadow story overcomes, at least temporarily, the primary narrative: "At last he's asleep. When she's certain of this, she lifts herself from the bed and carefully, quietly withdraws. As she closes the door, something in the flow of her own mind appalls her, and she stops, stands in the dim hallway, frozen in a kind of wonder: she had been thinking in an abstract way, almost idly, as though it had nothing to do with her, about how people will go to such lengths leaving a room—wishing not to disturb, not to awaken, a loved one."

The simple act of closing a door, given all that has come before it, becomes the means by which the inevitable surprise breaks through the story that has attempted to dominate it. Of course, this implied reawakening of affection may only be temporary, but it occupies the final position of the story, and the narrative resonates with its arrival. It's an arrival that's inevitable, and I've tried to highlight the moves that Bausch executes to subtly make us aware on a subconscious level that this ending is coming. He give us just a few glimpses of it and then gives us enough reason to forget it. It's a sleight of hand, a game of peekaboo, a promise and a subversion, a covert operation that becomes clear to us only after we've reached the end and lived within the reverberation of that surprise that's been waiting for us all along, a surprise that gives us more truth, hits upon more layers of experience and emotional response that coexist in that final tableau.

Framing the Story

A story sets its parameters with the writer's first step onto the page. The opening line starts to frame the material that the story will take on. Frank O'Connor, when asked how he began a short story, said: "It's the design of the story that to me is most important, the thing that tells you there's a bad gap in the narrative here and you really ought to fill that up in some way or another. I'm always looking at the design of a story, not the treatment." Consider, then, the opening of O'Connor's "Guests of the Nation":

> At dusk the big Englishman, Belcher, would shift his long legs out of the ashes and say, "Well, chums, what about it?" and Noble or me would say "All right, chum" (for we had picked up some of their curious expressions), and the little Englishman, Hawkins, would light the lamp and bring out the cards. Sometimes Jeremiah Donovan would come up and supervise the game and get excited over Hawkins's cards, which he always played badly, and shout at him as if he was one of our own. "Ah, you divil, you, why didn't you play the tray?"

The story thus begins to frame itself as it presents its major players: the Irishmen, Noble and Donovan; the narrator; and their English prisoners, Belcher and Hawkins, captured during the Irish battle for independence in 1922. Not only does the story present the main characters, it also announces the premise and poses the question of what will happen when the Irishmen, who have become fond of the English prisoners, are ordered to take them out and execute them. The story is already moving toward its final sentence in which the narrator, recalling the execution, says, "And anything that happened me afterwards, I never felt the same about again." By this point everything within the parameters of the story and its premise has been tested and put to use. The story never veers away from its focus, never strays from the parameters firmly announced in its opening.

At some point in the draft of a story, a writer usually becomes aware of these dramatic boundaries, or the frame of action that focuses the material. At yet another point in the composing process (and this may not come until many drafts later), the writer understands what the story is about within that frame of action, which is to say that the writer begins to sense what he or she has come to the material to explore. The writer becomes aware of what Poe called the unity of effect of the good short story, every element contributing to its overall intent.

Working within the parameters set in motion by the opening, the writer views the characters and their situations from as many different angles as possible so that by the end the reader feels that there's nothing left to be examined. The writer has gotten everything out of the framed material that he or she possibly can.

The lesson, then, is one of establishing the parameters and then staying within the framed area through a sequence of events that chips away at the material until something clearly defined and irrevocable emerges. Take your time. Let the material and the characters create the action of the story, action that will become increasingly complicated as it creates unexpected effects that then require further action until, finally, no other action can be taken. Write to the point within the material beyond which your main character will never feel the same again.

Character and Incident

When I was a kid, I thought time sometimes crept by so slowly. Now, of course, not so much. As a kid, I was good at making my inner thoughts known to anyone nearby, especially my parents when we were doing something grown-up like visiting their friends or shopping or an endless number of activities for which I had little patience. I was very verbal about how bored I was, how eager to go home, how thirsty, how hungry, how miserable. I had no filter between what I thought and what I said. I was a kid. I hadn't learned to keep things to myself.

I'm thinking about this today as I consider how our main characters register the way the world shifts around them. A large part of that world, of course, is the relationship that the character has with someone else and/or with a situation central to the narrative. The evolution of the character relationship is connected to the shifts in the central dramatic situation. As Henry James said: "What is character but the determination of incident? What is incident but the illustration of character?" So, the character, through his or her actions, creates incident, and that incident reveals more of the character.

It seems to me that a good story gives us something to hold onto in its opening, something that the story will hold onto throughout as well, this focal point to which everything in the story will connect. Consider this opening to Anton Chekhov's "The Lady with the Pet Dog," as translated by Avrahm Yarmolinsky:

A new person, it was said, had appeared on the esplanade: a lady with a pet dog. Dmitry Dmitrich Gurov, who had spent a fortnight at Yalta and had got used to the place, had also begun to take an interest in new arrivals. As he sat in Vernet's confectionery shop, he saw, walking on the esplanade, a fair-haired young woman of medium height, wearing a beret; a white Pomeranian was trotting behind her.

And afterwards he met her in the public garden and in the square several times a day. She walked alone, always wearing the same beret and always with the white dog; no one knew who she was and everyone called her simply "the lady with the pet dog."

"If she is here alone without husband or friends," Gurov reflected, "it wouldn't be a bad thing to make her acquaintance."

And so the heart of the story announces itself: Gurov's attraction to the lady with the pet dog. As the story unfolds and their relationship deepens and becomes complicated, Gurov registers each shift and turn, and because he does, we do too. We know exactly where to place our attention because Gurov knows where to place his.

Notice how this also works in a first-person narrative such as Amy Bloom's "Silver Water":

My sister's voice was like mountain water in a silver pitcher; the clear, blue beauty of it cools you and lifts you up beyond your heat, beyond your body. After we went to see *La Traviata*, when she was fourteen and I was twelve, she elbowed me in the parking lot and said, "Check this out." And she opened her mouth unnaturally wide and her voice came out, so crystalline and bright, that all the departing operagoers stood frozen by their cars, unable to take out their keys or open their doors until she had finished and then they cheered like hell.

That's what I like to remember and that's the story I told to all of her therapists. I wanted them to know her, to know that who they saw was not all there was to see. That before the constant tinkling of commercials and fast-food jingles, there had been Puccini and Mozart and hymns so sweet and mighty, you expected Jesus to come down off his cross and clap. That before there was a mountain of Thorazined fat, swaying down the halls in nylon maternity tops and sweat-pants, there had been the prettiest girl in Arrandale Elementary School, the belle of Landmark Junior High. Maybe there were other pretty girls, but I didn't see them. To me, Rose, my beautiful blond defender, my guide to Tampax and my mother's moods, was perfect.

We know from this opening that we're to hold onto the relationship between the narrator and her sister, Rose, and the way that relationship shifts through a series of complications because of Rose's delicate mental health. Because the narrator knows what's important in the story, we do too.

It may seem like such a small thing, this focusing, something barely worth mentioning, but I think it's wise to consider how to connect your readers with your characters and their situations through the opening of a piece of fiction. While putting your main character into action, don't forget to show your readers how he or she processes the world around him or her and how he or she registers the shifts in the dramatic situation and the character relationships. Even while "showing," don't be fearful of a little "telling," or a lot of telling, depending on what the story requires.

I Didn't Expect That

I'm reading Russell Banks's story collection *A Permanent Member of the Family*, and a few of the stories have reminded me of a good lesson for the writer of short fiction.

One of our challenges is to make our stories fresh. To do that, we need to consider how we handle our material. How do we spin the premise of a story to make it seem unlike any other story that a reader might have read?

Let's take the premises of three of Banks's stories. In "Former Marine" an aging father who's lost his job at an auction house, decides to start robbing banks. In "Christmas Party" a man attends a holiday tree–decorating party at the home of his ex-wife and her new husband. Finally, in "Transplant" a man receives a new heart. Frankly, if these were elevator pitches, I doubt there'd be much to excite us. In fact, the stories would promise to be tired and worn, clichéd plots full of sentimentality and melodrama. As Banks proves, it's not the premise that makes a story; it's what the writer does with that premise that counts.

The aging father in "Former Marine" has three sons. One of them is a prison guard, one is a city policeman, and the other is a state trooper. When they find out that their father is robbing banks, the moral complexity of the premise deepens, as Banks brings the tale to a dramatic end. The ex-husband in "Christmas Party" happens into the room where a young woman is trying to get the newly adopted baby of the ex-wife and her new husband to sleep. When Harold, the ex-husband, picks up the baby and starts moving toward the door as if to spirit the child away, a strange and interesting darkness rises up in the story. In "Transplant" the recipient of the new heart receives a request from the donor's wife, via the surgeon, to meet with him. The recipient agrees. It's not an unusual request, but no one can predict what the donor's wife will ask when the meeting finally occurs. She wants to listen to her dead husband's heart beating in the recipient's chest. She has a stethoscope with her for that purpose. The story ends with the slightly strange but very human moment of the donor's wife and the recipient atop a hill. She has the bell of the stethoscope pressed to his chest, and after a while she lets it drop away. Then she rests her ear against his chest, and the two of them hold each other as she goes on listening to the heart that once beat inside her husband's chest. The end of this story is handled with just the right balance of emotion and restraint, and it becomes unforgettable.

The lesson in all this? When conceiving a story, we're wise to turn a premise toward the thing that would be least expected but also believable. That little tweak will help us create memorable plots. An aging man robs banks? Give him sons who work in law enforcement. A man attends his ex-wife's holiday party? Let him almost steal her child. A heart transplant recipient gets a request to meet from the donor's wife? Give her a stethoscope and a desire to listen to that heart beating. The least expected turn freshens the premise by making it just a little strange while also making it extremely familiar and human. Banks makes such leaps possible because he stays open to spontaneity. He says, "With a short story, I never know where I'm going until I get there." We can invite this space of not knowing by asking ourselves what we'd least expect to happen with each premise for a story and then seeing if we can make that unexpected turn convincing.

One Way to Structure a Memoir

On a snowy night in 1965 my parents and I made a five-hour drive from our suburban Chicago home to the downstate hospital where my grandmother was dying. We'd left our farm and our extended family behind in order for my mother to take a teaching position in Oak Forest, Illinois, a move, as she later confided to me, she thought unnecessary, a move that had been solely my father's idea. I'm not sure we ever felt like we belonged in Chicagoland. On that February night in 1965 we had to make our way back home. That became one of the moments I wanted to include in my first memoir, *From Our House*.

I structured the memoir with a narrative arc that used geography as an organizing principle. The narrative broke down nicely into three distinct sections: my early childhood on our farm in southeastern Illinois and the event that led to our leaving for Oak Forest; our years in Oak Forest and our poor attempts to fit in before deciding to move back downstate; our return to southeastern Illinois and the life we finally accepted there. Beginning, middle, end.

Beneath that narrative arc, though, was the complicated story of the farming accident that cost my father both of his hands, the anger he brought into our home and the difficulties between us, and our eventual reconciliation.

Memoirs are not only about what happened; they're also about the complications between people and how they rub up against one another. I decided to let each chapter of *From Our House* feature a single event that provided a turning point in my family's story. The chapter that opens with the drive we made on that snowy night uses my grandmother's death for its narrative center, but it also uses that event as a catalyst for a shift in my relationship with my father. The event, then, is working on the level of plot as well as characterization.

I was nine years old in February 1965, and once we arrived at the hospital downstate and found out that my father's mother, my Grandma Martin, had passed, we stayed with my aunt and uncle while funeral arrangements were made. On the morning of the funeral I found myself stricken with an inexpressible sadness. I refused to get out of bed. My uncle tried to coax me, but still I refused. Finally, my father came into the room, and I braced myself for his anger, which was the custom between us. He surprised me by lying down on the bed with me. The pressure of a plot event often causes someone to act out of character. That person, then, becomes more alive to us, more complicated. The newness that we see in him or her demands our response. While my father and I were lying on the bed, a rooster on my uncle's farm began to crow, even though it was well past daybreak:

"Hear that?" my father said. "Mr. Rooster's all mixed up. He must have slept through the dawn. He must have been an old lazy bones. Now he's too late."

I heard my father's voice break, and it startled me. I pulled my head out from under my pillow and saw him lying on his back, his eyes closed, his hooks clasped on top of his stomach. "When I die," he had said, as we had left my grandma's wake, "everyone will come just to see if they bury me with these hooks." It was, perhaps, the first time I understood that my father, so much older than my friends' fathers, might die while I was young. And though he was the man who whipped me, he was my father, and freedom from him would carry with it an everlasting guilt, a regret that we hadn't found a way to love each other more.

It was impossible for me to snuggle in close to him, because of his hooks, but I moved as close as I could and felt the heat from his body.

"We have to go," he said. "You know that, don't you?"

27

I didn't answer. In a while, he would ask me if I was ready, and we would rise and go to the funeral home. But for the moment, we lay there, the two of us alone, while the rooster crowed again and my father said, "Good morning," as if we were just then waking to a new day.

When we write a memoir, we might want to first think about what's unresolved. For me it was my father's accident and how that affected our relationship. Then we might identify a particular time period in which this unresolved thing was most relevant. I knew my memoir would begin with my father's accident and anger and end with his baptism when I was sixteen years old. Once we have that basic framework, we can start recalling the events that brought about turning points in the relationship most central to the book.

Two arcs, then: one of plot and one of characterization. In memoir what happens always presses up against the people involved. We reveal ourselves and others through our responses to the events of our lives. Sometimes the events are large, as was the case with my grandmother's death, but sometimes within those large moments we find the smaller moments that still resonate even though years have passed. I wouldn't get out of bed. My father lay down beside me and allowed himself to be vulnerable. I had to respond.

Organizing the Memoir

When writing a memoir, we're faced with issues of selectivity as we decide what to include and what to leave out. It seems to me that it's a mistake to try to include everything from our lives; that's what autobiographies are for. Memoirs are different animals. They work best when focused on a specific arc of time or when they're organized around a particular consideration. Think of Tobias Wolff's *This Boy's Life*, with its narrative beginning at the time immediately following his parents' divorce and ending with his escape from his abusive stepfather as he leaves for prep school in the East. Consider, too, the fact that Wolff later wrote another memoir, *In Pharaoh's Army*, which focused on his service in Vietnam. Each book has a clearly defined arc of time.

Then consider a book like Matthew Gavin Frank's *Preparing the Ghost* that takes as its center the story of a giant squid and uses it as a point of departure. The book is driven partly by multiengined narratives but also by lyric association, by lists, by imagination. At its center the book is a meditation on issues of obsession, mystery, and mythmaking. Although the shape of the book is what some might consider loose, it's precisely that shapelessness that brings into focus the colossal size of our lives. The book has the central metaphor of the giant squid to anchor us as we follow its leaps and turns.

Two very different approaches to memoir, each of them completely valid and appropriate for each writer's intention. Wolff wants to tell us a story of a particular section of his life; Frank wants to tell us stories inside stories while letting the details lead him hither and thither but always with a particular consideration in mind. Each writer's approach is organic to his aesthetic of what a memoir should be and what effect it should create for the reader.

The wonderful thing about creative nonfiction, even within the specific form of the memoir, is that there's room for so many different aesthetics. We should never let someone else's determine our own. Know what your own experience was—a logical progression from point A to point B, perhaps, or a mosaic of events, associations, meditations—and find the form and shape that will best allow your reader to have the same experience.

The Layers of Memoir

This is a Passage of Fact and Nostalgia

As we make the turn toward Thanksgiving, I'm thinking about my mother's side of the family and how each year we gathered for a holiday meal at one house or the other. My mother always brought a chiffon cake. My Aunt Myrtle made bread pudding. My Aunt Mildred made coleslaw. My cousin's wife Gerri made baked beans. My other cousin's wife, Arlene, made a Jell-O salad. There was turkey and ham and mashed potatoes and gravy and noodles and dressing. The men ate while the women served them, and only after the men were finished did the women sit down to eat. Pumpkin pie, pecan pie, angel food cake with fruit salad, and, of course, that bread pudding. Hot dinner rolls and glasses of iced tea and steaming cups of coffee. The kids ate at a card table in the garage if the weather was warm enough or in the living room if it wasn't. I remember when I got old enough to join the men at their table, my Uncle Richard said I would sit by him, and he proceeded to fill my plate with food. Some I wanted, and some I didn't. Never mind, he told me, it's all good for you. The talk around the table was about farm crops and deer hunting. My uncles and my older cousins told stories, jokes. They laughed easily and loudly. My Uncle Homer, whose house often hosted us, was a nervous sort. He spent the afternoon fidgeting. My Uncle Harry smoked Camel cigarettes, the nonfiltered kind, and was always sneaking back into the kitchen after dinner for another slice of pie, another cup of coffee. He and my Aunt Mildred and my cousin Melanie lived an hour north, in Charleston, Illinois, a college town. Harry was a former newspaper editor who went to work for Eastern Illinois University as their director of public information. He was the sibling who had left the farm for the city, and I liked him tremendously because he gave me books for Christmas. Even then, his life seemed to be the one I wanted for myself.

This Is a Passage of Incident

One Thanksgiving, after the men had eaten, my Uncle Homer said something that my Uncle Harry thought was racist. This happened during the late 1960s, when so much of the country was on edge because of the Vietnam War and the civil rights movement. I'm not sure that I ever knew exactly what Homer said, but I still remember the twisted feeling inside my stomach when I heard the loud voices coming from the living room and when I realized those voices were coming from my uncles. Just like that, my family became strange to me, defamiliarized. Something was happening that hadn't happened before—this argument between my backward-thinking Uncle Homer and my more progressive Uncle Harry—and there I was, maybe thirteen years old, taking my first steps toward trying to figure out the sort of man I wanted to be. Harry told Homer in no uncertain terms what he thought of his bigotry. Homer wouldn't back down. That's when Harry told my aunt that they were leaving, and they did. They gathered up my cousin Melanie, got into their car, and drove away.

This Is a Passage of Thinking

That night I couldn't go to sleep because I kept replaying the events of the afternoon, struggling to make sense of it all. My uncles, who had always gotten along so well, had been so angry with each other that one of them stormed away. I liked my Uncle Homer, but now I didn't know what to make of him. He'd said something so ugly that my Uncle Harry felt he had no recourse but to remove himself and my aunt and cousin from Homer's house. I believed in equality, and the more I thought about what had happened, the more I admired Harry for the stand he'd made and for his unwillingness to tolerate Homer's racism. I wanted to believe that given the chance, I would have done exactly what

Harry did. I'd always admired him, but from that day forward I sought to emulate him.

This Is a Passage of Connection
and Questioning

Over forty years later my cousin Melanie and her husband dissolved their marriage, and my cousin fell in love with a black man. Harry refused to meet him. He forbade Melanie from bringing him to visit. He essentially closed his daughter, whom he had always loved and protected fiercely, out of his life. When I learned about it, the first thing I thought of was that Thanksgiving when Harry had stood up to Homer because of his racial intolerance, and now here he was, Harry, demonstrating the same behavior. I'll never know how to reconcile these two memories of my uncle. All I can do is accept the fact that those contradictions exist. I'll always wonder whether his encroaching Alzheimer's influenced his behavior or whether it was easier for him to talk the talk than to walk the walk. Did his ethics take a backward step when it came to his own daughter? He told Melanie he had always wished for so much more for her. When Melanie proposed that she and the love of her life meet my aunt and uncle somewhere for dinner, she was met with resistance. "What would you say about that?" she asked Harry, and Harry said, "I'd say no." I loved my uncle dearly. Now that he's gone, how do I make room for this image of him? All I can do is accept the fact that we're all made up of contradictions, even the people we idolize.

This Is What I Want to Say
about Writing Memoir

Fact without incident, thought, connection to something larger, interrogation, and speculation is often merely nostalgia. Memoir exists to take us further into the future, not to keep us rooted in the past. It's the layers of detail, event, reflection, and the writer's mind and heart at work that create whatever meaning we make of experience.

I Was Wearing Them the Day

Touchstone Moments and Details for the Fiction Writer

I've always been interested in the question of where the fiction writer finds material. I've always been particularly interested in how the autobiographical gets transformed into fiction. My curiosity comes not from a prurient interest in the lives of writers but more from a desire to provide my students a way to increase the urgency and intensity in their stories, to write about people and events and objects that matter deeply to the writers themselves, even if those characters and their actions and the things they possess are pure inventions. Still, I believe writers create more memorable works when they either consciously or unconsciously make space for their own lives within their fictions. That's why I often begin a fiction workshop with a nonfiction writing activity, one that invites the writers to recall specific moments from their pasts that were full of emotional complexity. Moments of simultaneous love and hate, fear and courage, pride and shame, or any other binary of opposites. I call these "touchstone moments," ones that we fiction writers can tap into on an unconscious level during the writing of a story or novel and, by so doing, create a more resonant work.

I'm also interested in the use we fiction writers make of the objects that populate our invented worlds. Flannery O'Connor, in *Mysteries and Manners*, says, "In good fiction, certain of the details will accumulate meaning from the action of the story itself, and when this happens they become symbolic in the way they work." She cites her own story "Good Country People" as an example. The story of a spiritually and physically maimed young woman who wears a wooden leg that ends up being stolen

34

by a traveling Bible salesman. As O'Connor points out, writing about this story in *Mysteries and Manners,* the theft reveals the young woman's deeper affliction to her, the affliction that comes from the absence of faith. The Bible salesman says to her as he's about to leave: "You ain't so smart. I been believing in nothing ever since I was born!" The detail of the wooden leg, then, works within the plot of the story while at the same time expanding it thematically. If we fill our fictional worlds with concrete details and then make them a significant part of the action, we not only hasten the plot along, we also complicate the thematic concerns of a narrative in a rich and interesting way.

Let's try a writing exercise that's meant to invite you to access one of those touchstone moments from the past so it'll be there at your disposal anytime you want to tap into its emotional complexity in your fiction. This exercise should also allow you to think about the way concrete objects acquire meaning through action.

1. Make a list of shoes that you remember wearing as a child. Go as far back in memory as you can.
2. Which pair of shoes on your list is resonating most strongly for you, probably because it's connected in some way to an emotionally complex moment from your childhood?
3. Using those shoes as your object, begin to freewrite with the words "I was wearing them the day . . . ." Narrate a moment from your past in which you felt contradictory emotions.

That's all there is to it. Tell a story from your past and feel the layers of emotion that you felt then, that you still feel when you recall it. Let that complicated moment fill you. Know that it's always there to help you create more resonant moments in your fiction, not necessarily replications of your experiences but containers for the complicated come and go of our lives at the ready for your use with created characters and events.

Yogi Berra and the Art of Flash Nonfiction

I remember a story about Yogi Berra trying to explain the fine art of hitting a baseball to another player and then realizing that he really couldn't explain it. "Let me show you," he said, and he proceeded to demonstrate. Yogi was also known to say at some point, "How can you hit and think at the same time?"

I'm thinking about this in connection with the flash form of creative nonfiction. Let's say we're talking about 750 words or fewer, the size of essays that our friends at *Brevity* publish. Believe me, there are plenty of folks who are smarter about this form than I, but I'll do my best to make what I hope will be some useful points, and maybe, like Yogi, I'll even try to show you.

To write flash nonfiction, you have to:

1. Get comfortable with not knowing. When I start a piece of flash nonfiction, I feel as if I'm a horse who has blinders on preventing me from seeing anything extraneous. I can only see as far as the sentence I'm writing takes me. I don't want to know where the piece is going. I want to be surprised when I get there.

2. Proceed with urgency. There's no time to get comfortable. Writing flash nonfiction is like being pushed into a river, one with a strong current. You have to survive. Every movement you make means something. It's life or death. Better start swimming. Better keep it up. The flash form demands this intensity even if the subject matter is quiet. You can't waste a single word.

3. Let the voice guide you. Others may see this differently, but for me writing flash nonfiction has always been a voice-driven enterprise. Sometimes I find a communal voice that sweeps the essay along; at other times I find an intimate, vulnerable personal voice that does the same work. A piece of flash nonfiction is in many ways a musical composition. It's important to be aware of the sounds your words are making and to use those sounds to take you where you're meant to be.

4. *Be brutal.* You have to be willing to restrain yourself while you're urgently writing. There's no time for explanation or much exposition. Flash nonfiction lives in the present moment even if you're writing about something that's long past. Remember that horse with the blinders? No time to notice what's around you. Stay grounded in what's immediate. Keep moving.

5. *Be open.* To me being open involves being willing to think in terms of opposites. I might begin a piece with a voice of certainty, for example, as I do in my essay "Talk Big": "Nights like this—a Friday night at last call after too much Pabst, and Jack, and Wild Turkey, and Seven and Sevens—we talk big. Why wouldn't we? We know who we are—the lowlifes, the no-accounts, the pissants, the stumblebums. All liquored up. Ten foot tall and bulletproof."

From the first line I'm on the lookout for the moment in the essay when the pressure of language, narrative, and imagery will turn that certainty into something that's quite the opposite. This, after a violent death, is the ending of the essay:

Afraid to be alone, afraid to shut our mouths, let our tongues go dead, our words dry up.
What'll we be then?
Scared shitless.
Scared to death.

This is the place I didn't know I was headed when the essay began.
I often rely on the compression of narrative, the urgency of language, the attention to details, to create an organic moment of surprise, a moment of resonance. A piece of flash nonfiction

can't be quiet at the end. It can make a quiet sound, but it has to make an unforgettable noise in your readers' hearts and minds. You have 750 words to make sure that no reader will ever forget the end of that essay.

Writing flash nonfiction is like something else Yogi Berra said: "You've got to be very careful if you don't know where you're going because you might not get there."

Mad Libs for Creative Nonfiction

I designed a new writing exercise not too long ago, and contrary to what a good teacher should have done (stating the objective of the exercise before leading the students through it), I purposely eliminated that step and jumped right in. I didn't want the students to write toward an objective, thereby thinking too much about the purpose of their responses to my cues. Instead, I wanted them to be open to leaps and associations and surprises and the texture such things can lend to a piece of creative nonfiction.

Now I'm sharing this exercise with you:

1. Make a list of three adjectives. Any three. Don't think too hard. Just do it.
2. Make a list of three objects that have recently become "unforgettable" to you in some way. Three objects from the current time or the recent past that you can't get out of your head.
3. Make a list of three abstractions but try to avoid nouns that could also be transitive verbs. Nothing that could be turned into a statement such as "I love *x*," or "I hate *y*." Stick with things like *limbo* or *harmony*.
4. Choose an adjective from your list, an object, and an abstraction. Do it in that order. Add a preposition or an article as necessary. Write the title of your essay (e.g., "Pretty Dog Leash in Limbo"). Note: now that you know you're creating a title, feel free to switch out any of the words for others on your lists.
5. Write a few lines about the object you've chosen. Why have you been thinking about it lately? Give us a context for why this object is important to you.

6. Write a few lines that evoke the abstraction you've chosen without naming it. How does the abstraction convey your emotional response to the object? In what way does thinking about the object leave you unsettled, uncertain, or whatever your emotional response turns out to be?

7. Write a few lines that evoke the adjective you've chosen without naming it. Give us a sense of its relationship to the object. Is it ironic, for example, or genuine?

8. Write a few lines about another object, story, or memory that comes to you right now. We're working with free association here. Look for words or phrases or images that subtly connect to what you've already written. If you need a prompt, here's one: "When I think of that dog leash, I remember [fill in the blank with another object, a story, a memory]."

9. Make a direct statement about where the second object, story, or memory takes you in your thinking. Here's a prompt: "I begin [or began] to think about [fill in the blank however you'd like]." The emphasis with this last step is to let the texture of the writing invite an abstract thought, conclusion, question, or speculation, thereby allowing the central line of inquiry of the essay to grow organically from what precedes it.

My students, in our post-writing debriefing, talked about how the exercise led them to unexpected connections, became a process of discovery, forced them to "push through" material that was a bit uncomfortable for them, and in general led them to things they wouldn't have gotten to otherwise. I'm hoping this exercise will be helpful for those writers who want to write in forms that aren't predominantly driven by narrative and who are more interested in dealing with recent material rather than the distant past.

Enough about Me, Tell Me
What You Think about Me

For years I've noticed a tendency for beginning writers of personal narratives to forget to make room for the other actors on the stage and to forget that memoirs take place in particular settings and at particular time periods that express particular values. I call this tendency the "Enough about Me, Tell Me What You Think about Me" syndrome. These writers are in love with the sound of their own voices. They believe themselves to be, to borrow from a popular beer commercial, "the most interesting people in the world." I'm having a bit of fun here because I don't think that their narcissism is intentional. It's merely the result of a lack of storytelling technique that will correct itself over time and with practice.

When I read a memoir, I want to feel like I'm a participant in a life. I don't want to be kept in the wings, watching. I want to be onstage living what the people in the memoir are living. The narcissistic approach keeps readers at a distance rather than immersed in the events. Although we're certainly interested in the sensibility of the narrator, we can begin to feel claustrophobic if he or she forgets to take a look outside that self. Although I love and value the art of reflection and thinking on the page that takes place in a good memoir, I confess to starting to lose interest if I'm asked to spend too much time inside the writer's head. The world starts to close down for me rather than open up. We need to make room for that world, not to diminish ourselves but to make ourselves larger by seeing what it means for us to interact with this person, this detail, this place, this time period, this action.

As I said earlier, I believe that this unintentional narcissistic approach is actually a deficiency of technique problem. Its symptoms include a lack of dialogue, a lack of detail, and a lack of action. It can easily be cured with a writing activity, which I prescribe for all of us now.

1. Select a lost object from your childhood, one that you've never forgotten, one that you wish you still had. My grandmother had a ladybug pin cushion when I was a child, and to this day I remember that she kept a Charles Percy campaign button stuck to it. Percy was the Republican candidate for governor in my home state of Illinois in 1964; he narrowly lost to the incumbent, Democrat Otto Kerner. My mother's family was Republican; my father was a staunch Democrat. I've always wondered what my grandmother thought about my mother's marriage to my father, an event that took place when my mother was forty-one, and the pin cushion and the Percy campaign button invite me to think about that. So, what's your object?

   Spend some time writing from this prompt: "I remember . . . ." Perhaps you'll hit upon a scene in which you're watching yourself as a child looking at this object or handling it, or maybe you'll remember what it was like to watch someone else using it. The important thing is to describe what you see, hear, smell, taste, touch, as you travel back in memory.

2. Daydream yourself into a specific memory. It might be one that involves your object, or it might be one that it suggests. If the power of association takes you away from the object, trust that you're meant to follow. I might recall, for example, the evening my father and my uncle, my mother's brother, got into a heated argument over politics and how strange it seemed to hear these men, who genuinely liked each other, raising their voices and saying things like "Herbert Hoover ruined the farmer!"

or "Spend, spend, spend. That's all a Democrat wants!"
What are the people in your memory saying?

3. My uncle finally got up from his chair that evening and
said to my aunt: "Get your coat, Myrtle. We're leaving."
What happened after that? My father, still angry, rehash-
ing the argument, his face red as he paced about our
kitchen, where my mother, whose views were the same
as my uncle's, cleared the coffee cups and dessert dishes
from the table and began to wash them, not saying a
word. What actions take place in your memory?

In order to pay attention to detail, dialogue, and characters
in action, you'll have to look outside the self, and you'll write a
scene in which you look at the larger world that may be social (a
gathering of relatives), cultural (at a time and in a place where
manners were supposed to always trump what one really thought),
and political (at a time in the 1960s when our country's political
climate was changing).

In all honesty I've never thought of myself as a political writer
or a cultural critic or a social commentator. But really, as I hope
my ladybug pin cushion has shown, any writer of memoir is all
three of these things. The small details of a life contain the social,
the cultural, and/or the political.

Shrinking a Novel

I just got back from teaching a workshop on the novel at the Vermont College of Fine Arts Postgraduate Writers' Conference. I had six first-time novelists in the workshop, and I'd seen about twenty-five pages of each manuscript before we all arrived in Montpelier. Some people had complete drafts of their novels, and some were still working toward that end. Each book was compelling and glorious in its own way. What in the heck could I do in our five days together to make any difference for these six writers?

It's been my experience that my own early efforts with the novel form are attempts to find the shape of the book and to fully understand what I'm trying to do with the material. My first drafts are very, very messy. When I teach a novel workshop at a conference, it's my goal to send the writers away with a clearer idea of what they're exploring and the structure they're building that will best house that exploration.

So, we talked about characterization, structure, detail, point of view, and language. I made suggestions for writing exercises, and I told my novelists that they should use any one of them that they preferred to either revise a troublesome section or to create something new that they sensed should be a part of the manuscript. They'd have their chance to share this work on our last day together.

Somewhere along the way I got a crazy idea. We were looking at Stuart Dybek's piece of flash fiction "Sunday at the Zoo." I love using that story to look at narrative structure. The compressed form is like an X-ray. It makes the bones of the structure stand out more clearly. I found myself thinking, why not compress the novel by asking folks to use their material to imitate the Dybek story. A couple of my students did just that, to stunning effects. Their pieces of flash fiction required them to focus on what was really important in their novels. It asked them to make choices. It led them to aspects of the material they hadn't considered. They more clearly defined the movement of their narratives. They found the right narrative voice. They wrote with more specificity and urgency. Listening to them read those pieces of flash fiction, I felt that they were much more intimate with the worlds of their novels. I felt their urgent need to tell their stories.

So, what conclusions can we draw from this? Perhaps writing in a short form can help us think about what really matters to us in the novels we're drafting or have drafted. Perhaps this compression can show us the way our novels want to move and can also make the shape of the book more clear. Take any piece of flash fiction that you'd like to use, as long as its aesthetic is in line with that of your novel. If your novel is heavily narrative, then the Dybek story will do nicely. If your novel is more contemplative and interested in exploring a character's interior life, à la *Mrs. Dalloway*, then perhaps a different story, maybe Woolf's "Kew Gardens," might be a better choice. Use whatever story you choose as a model. Identify the artistic choices that the author has made in the construction of that story. Then fit the material of your novel to its form. See what the process has to teach you about the work you're doing or have already done. Thomas Keneally, author of *Schindler's List* and many other fine books, talks about how he has to find the cookie cutter for each of his novels—in other words, the form to which everything will stick. Perhaps this exercise with the shorter form is one way to help the novelist find that cookie cutter.

Preparing the Final Scene
by Avoiding Conflict

I return to Richard Bausch's story "The Fireman's Wife." To refresh your memory, let me say that the story is about Jane, who is close to leaving her marriage to Martin. At the end of the story Martin has been injured while fighting a fire and has come home to find Jane's bag packed. Because of his injury, she doesn't leave that night. She gets him settled in bed, and the next morning she listens to his attempts to talk about why she shouldn't leave him. Then she walks outside. At this point Bausch does some interesting things with landscape and the past:

> Later, while he sleeps on the sofa, she wanders outside and walks down to the end of the driveway. The day is sunny and cool, with little cottony clouds—the kind of clear day that comes after a storm. She looks up and down the street. Nothing is moving. A few houses away someone has put up a flag, and it flutters in a stray breeze. This is the way it was, she remembers, when she first lived here—when she first stood on this sidewalk and marveled at how flat the land was, how far it stretched in all directions. Now she turns and makes her way back to the house, and then she finds herself in the garage. It's almost as if she's saying goodbye to everything, and, as this thought occurs to her, she feels a little stir of sadness. Here, on the work table, side by side under the light from the one window, are Martin's model airplanes. He won't be able to work on them again for weeks. The light reveals the miniature details, the crevices and curves on which he lavished such care, gluing and sanding

and painting. The little engines are lying on a paper towel at one end of the table. They smell just like real engines, and they're shining with lubrication. She picks one of them up and turns it in the light, trying to understand what he might see in it that could require such time and attention. She wants to understand him. She remembers that when they dated, he liked to tell her about flying those planes, and his eyes would widen with excitement. She remembers that she liked him best when he was glad that way. She puts the little engine down, thinking how people change. She knows she's going to leave him, but just for this moment, standing among these things, she feels almost at peace about it. She has, after all, no need to hurry. And as she steps out on the lawn, she realizes she can take the time to think clearly about when and where; she can even change her mind. But she doesn't think she will.

"The Fireman's Wife" is a story that exhibits an extraordinary measure of restraint at the moment of climax. Rather than rushing ahead toward resolution, Bausch slows down and delivers a more nuanced portrait of a marriage in trouble. The drama happens at the level of character more so than the completion of action, and that's because of Bausch's sensitive and extraordinary management of Jane's point of view.

So, with a similar objective in mind, I offer the following exercise. This might work best with a story that you've already drafted or are in the process of drafting, but it could also be useful for a story that you're thinking about writing.

1. Imagine a climactic moment for two of your characters, one that will bring them to a tipping point, a place where your point of view character might take an action that will change everything forever.
2. Have your point of view character walk away from the conflict.

3. Use the landscape and a detail that's specific to the other character to activate the point of view character's memory and to spark a divide within him or her as this character straddles the past life and the one that lies ahead.

The objective of the exercise is to see what you can find within your point of view character before he or she enters the final scene of the story. By creating a moment of pause, the final resolution makes a louder noise; even if it's fairly quiet in terms of action, it's very resonant in terms of what rises up in the main character. In the case of "The Fireman's Wife" Jane experiences a surprise that she never could have predicted. She returns to the house and checks on Martin, who is sleeping. Bausch then gives us the powerful last paragraph in which Jane, leaving the bedroom, realizes she's closing the door the way one would if they didn't want to bother a loved one.

A simple action like closing a door can lead to a resonant end if your point of view character is alert enough to the world around him or her—if the action draws out a crucial response, one the reader won't be able to forget.

Here We Are at the End

I'd like to offer some thoughts about ending a piece of fiction or nonfiction with resonance. Emily Dickinson said in an 1870 remark to Thomas Wentworth Higginson: "If I read a book and it makes my whole body so cold no fire can ever warm me, I know that is poetry. If I feel physically as if the top of my head were taken off, I know that is poetry. These are the only ways I know it. Is there any other way?" To me something always goes off at the end of a good piece of writing in a way that sends shockwaves through the reader. There are numerous ways to achieve this resonance. Here are but a few.

And it seemed as though in a little while the solution would be found, and then a new and glorious life would begin; and it was clear to both of them that the end was still far off, and that what was to be most complicated and difficult for them was only just beginning. ("The Lady with the Pet Dog" by Anton Chekhov)

Here we see an ending based on a simultaneous closing and opening. The two lovers, married to other people, long to be free from their "intolerable fetters." Notice how the glimmer of hope in the thought that they'd soon find a solution clangs up against the awareness of the difficulty that lies ahead. The sound, then, is resonant because hope and reality coexist. The story ends with the sound of two discordant notes—the hope for "a new and glorious life" vibrating against the troubled life they'll have to face.

❧

You think it's strange that you assumed you were the only boy hurt by that kiss in Mark's bedroom. But you see that Jared carries that day with him like you do; he carries a shame not very different from yours. Somehow you've shared a scar for this many years. You say to Jared that just knowing he remembers is enough. He thanks you and grabs you again. On your shoulder his hand feels a little like the warmth of comfort, and a little like the squeeze of danger. ("If You Knew Then What I Know Now" by Ryan Van Meter)

This piece of nonfiction about a boyhood hurt achieves its resonance by a leveling of a binary. Throughout the essay we've seen the writer as the victim and Jared as the bully. In this final move Van Meter allows Jared equal footing when he realizes that Jared has been scarred by the incident too. The last line resonates with ambivalence. Jared's hand feels like comfort, but it also feels like danger. Writers create this effect by practicing the art of empathy, of seeing something from inside the other.

❧

I move toward Eugene. "I will have something," I roar.

"Stand back," he shrieks, "I'll spit in your eye."

"I will have something. I will have terror. I will have drought. I bring the dearth. Famine's contagious. Also is thirst. Privation, privation, bareness, void. I dry up your glands, I poison your well."

He is choking, gasping, chewing furiously. He opens his mouth. It is dry. His throat is parched. There is sand on his tongue.

They moan. They are terrified, but they move up to see. We are thrown together. Slud, Frank, Clob, Mimmer, the others, John Williams, myself. I will not be reconciled, or

halve my hate. It's what I have, all I can keep. My bully's sour
solace. It's enough, I'll make do.

I can't stand them near me. I move against them. I shove
them away. I force them off. I press them, thrust them aside.
I push through. ("A Poetics for Bullies" by Stanley Elkin)

Elkin's short story resonates with force at the end. The narrator, Push the bully, persists. The end of the story builds to a cre-
scendo. It makes a loud sound. Notice how the final sentences
work to achieve this. Four short declarative sentences followed
by a variation, a momentary rest ("I press them, thrust them
aside") before climaxing with the final short sentence, "I push
through." That rest before the final push (pun intended) makes
all the difference in the resonant sound at the end.

But after I got them to leave and shut the door and turned
off the light it wasn't any good. It was like saying good-by to
a statue. After a while I went out and left the hospital and
walked back to the hotel in the rain. (*A Farewell to Arms* by
Ernest Hemingway)

Who better than Hemingway to illustrate the art of understate-
ment? Here, after the dramatic death of Catherine and her baby,
Hemingway chooses to leave us with the quietude of Frederick
walking back to his hotel in the rain. The stillness of that last sentence resonates because of the intensity of the dramatic action
that precedes it.

I hope these examples prove useful to you as you think about
how to end a piece so it resonates with your readers.

Taking Care at the End

The Art of Misdirection

Brian Hinshaw's brilliant piece of flash fiction "The Custodian" is told in two paragraphs. Here's the first one:

> The job would get boring if you didn't mix it up a little. Like this woman in 14-A, the nurses called her the mockingbird, start any song and this old lady would sing it through. Couldn't speak, couldn't eat a lick of solid food, but she sang like a house on fire. So for a kick, I would go in there with my mop and such, prop the door open with the bucket, and set her going. She was best at the songs you'd sing with a group—"Oh Susanna," campfire stuff. Any kind of Christmas song worked good too, and it always cracked the nurses if I could get her into "Let It Snow" during a heat spell. We'd try to make her to take up a song from the radio or some of the old songs with cursing in them, but she would never go for those. Although once I had her do "How Dry I Am" while Nurse Winchell fussed with the catheter.

In the opening we meet a narrator (I'm going to assume it's a man, though the story never specifies the gender) who works as a custodian in a health care facility. To keep the job from being too boring, he gets the patient in 14-A to sing, the only verbalization apparently that she's capable of. There's some lightness of tone in the opening. It's apparent in the language: "mix it up a little," "sang like a house on fire," "it always cracked the nurses." At the end of the first paragraph we learn that the custodian once had the woman sing "How Dry I Am" while a nurse attends to the patient's catheter. When I read this story aloud, people generally laugh at that line, and then in our conversation that follows, they admit to feeling guilty about laughing because they're aware that the custodian may be dehumanizing the patient. I'd suggest that we haven't been aware of the submerged story, the one that's quite opposite from the one suggested by the opening lines, but at the very end of the first paragraph that submerged story begins to rise.

Here's the second and final paragraph of the story:

Yesterday, her daughter or maybe granddaughter comes in while 14-A and I were partways into "Auld Lang Syne" and the daughter says "oh oh oh" like she had interrupted scintillating conversation and then she takes a long look at 14-A lying there in the gurney with her eyes shut and her curled-up hands, taking a cup of kindness yet. And the daughter looks at me the way a girl does at the end of an old movie and she says "my god," says "you're an angel," and now I can't do it anymore, can hardly step into her room.

Notice what happens with language in that first sentence. The immediate pause after *Yesterday* signals a shift in tone from the lightness of the first paragraph to the gravity of the second one. The submerged story, as it surfaces, requires a more contemplative tone. As that first sentence unwinds, it contains more than one pause, and actually we might argue that the second sentence is really a continuation of the first.

Of course, there's a great misreading in what the daughter thinks of the custodian. She thinks he's doing something good by bringing a few moments of regular life and joy to the patient by getting her to sing. The daughter sees this as a completely beneficent act on the part of the custodian. He knows, though, that his motive hasn't been beneficent at all but, instead, self-serving, a way of warding off the boredom. He feels so ashamed that he can't continue, can hardly step into 14-A, where the patient will no longer have the opportunity for that singing. Is that a good thing? A bad thing? Both? The answer becomes complicated, the way it always does at the end of a good story that captures some simultaneous loss and gain. Perhaps, the custodian's actions, though selfish in nature, actually did create something positive for the patient. Or perhaps his action was so wrong that it's a good thing that he's stopped. It seems to me that once the submerged story fully rises, it's impossible to privilege one interpretation over the other. A binary has been leveled, and the ending resonates with the complexity of truth made possible through Brian Hinshaw's art of misdirection. We thought we were reading a story about a custodian who had no thought of what he might be doing when he got the patient to sing, but really we were reading, as the ending proves, a story of a man coming to an awareness of how someone else interprets his action, choosing to think of him as an angel but at the cost of him never again wanting to get 14-A to sing. A very complicated human story has fully arrived through the scrim of a more simple story of self-interest.

At some point we all need to experience what it feels like when a narrative takes a surprising and resonant turn. We need to put into practice a story that begins leaning one direction, only to lean in the opposite direction at its end. The opposite story, or the submerged story, rises within the structure of the primary story, the one we think we're reading. The pressure of plot (notice how the third character, the daughter, becomes the final catalyst necessary for the submerged story to become visible) forces the submerged story to the top. Dramatic irony, in this case accomplished through the daughter's misreading, provides an opposite result to what the custodian intended, bringing him to a different view of himself and the world around him. That world changes in a profound way that resonates with readers. It's as if a gong sounds and the sound waves reverberate back through the story and on into the future beyond the story's end. Simply put, we can't forget it because it arrives in such a covert but totally genuine way.

If you'd like to put all of this into practice, think of a job that you had that could get boring or that you wanted to be done with. What did you do to "mix it up a little"? How can you imitate Hinshaw's story? Two paragraphs, one that establishes the surface story and then signals the submerged story beginning to rise at the end of the first paragraph and one that allows the submerged story to fully rise. How can you use a third character as a catalyst? How can you use a misreading to lead us to an ironic and resonant end?

PART 2 ❦ Characterization

There Were Three Little Pigs

People are individuals.
Yes, they may be expected to be a
particular way. But that doesn't mean
they're going to be that way.

—MARGARET ATWOOD

On a Mother's Birthday, a
Writer Loves the World

Today is my mother's birthday. She'd be 101 years old. She was a soft-spoken woman who put others before herself. Some may have thought her meek, but she had a fierce strength inside her that allowed her to endure the twists and turns her life took. She was a woman who knew how to endure, a woman of duty, but I hope she also knew how to thrive. I hope she had a million small graces that made her love her life.

I remember how she sat on the edge of my bed, nights when I had trouble falling asleep, and told me to count my blessings, to remind myself of everything that was good. She was a woman of great compassion and faith, and there's something in that forgiveness and belief that moves through the writer I've become.

A writer loves the world with all of his or her heart even while trying to make sense of its injustices, injuries, and conundrums. Why else do writers labor with words if not because we love the world around us? We hope for better; we mourn when the world and its people disappoint us. We believe in happiness and perfection even when we know that the former is inconsistent and the latter is impossible.

I'm always a bit taken aback whenever readers of my books start talking about how much they didn't like one of my characters. As far as I can tell, these readers are reacting to the imperfect nature of folks—to the stumbles and mistakes we all make along the way. It's not my job to judge my characters. It's my job to give them free will, to watch them get themselves into trouble, and to see what they'll do to try to redeem themselves. It's my job to understand the sources of my characters' behaviors.

I don't have to like what they do. I just have to know what leads them down certain paths. In the process I challenge myself to find some degree of empathy for them, no matter how much I dislike the choices that they make.

Everyone's life is imperfect. Our characters' lives are too. We should resist passing judgment on them, understanding, as we must, that we don't start our lives making mistakes. We start out in innocence. It's impossible to stay there, though. Things happen. Sometimes we find ourselves past the point where we can return. We all know that, which should make us more tolerant rather than less. I rarely heard my mother say a bad word about anyone. She was too busy believing in love.

Tightening the Screws

Putting Pressure on Our Characters

There's a moment in Tobias Wolff's story "An Episode in the Life of Professor Brooke" in which Brooke's colleague Riley asks him to tell him the worst things he's ever done. As I was walking upstairs to meet my MFA fiction workshop for the first time this semester, I was thinking about how in all good fiction we get the sense that the story or the novel really mattered to the writer—that the subject matter wasn't just chosen willy-nilly but instead exists because for whatever reason the writer *had* to work with it. We don't know why it matters to the writer, but we feel the urgency in the telling. I know that when my own drafts fail to interest or touch me, it's usually because I haven't figured out why I need to write about a particular situation or character.

I began yesterday's workshop by asking folks to consider how they would answer Riley's question if it were put to them. "What the worst thing you've ever done?" I told a story from my own experience (sure, I've done worst things than the moment I shared, but c'mon, do you really think I'd tell *everything*?) that happened when I was in the fifth grade. Our community was in the midst of a hepatitis outbreak, the kind that makes folks very, very sick, and it was known that the father of one of my classmates, April, who was a quiet, nervous girl, had been dramatically ill. One morning, before our lessons began, my teacher, Mrs. Malley, asked April how her father was doing. April said he was much, much better. I raised my hand. I said, "Isn't it true that people can die from hepatitis?" I intended to impress Mrs. Malley with my knowledge. I had no idea that my question would send April into a fit of choked sobs or that Mrs. Malley would give me a stern look that would make me shrivel up with shame. A lesson for the future writer: someone's intent can often produce the opposite result, and that sort of dramatic irony can lend resonance to a piece of fiction.

Wolff is a master of this sort of irony. Professor Brooke, who thinks of himself as a decent sort, can't help but sit in judgment of Riley. The story opens with this line: "Professor Brooke had no real quarrel with anyone in his department, but there was a Yeats scholar named Riley whom he could not bring himself to like." Right away, then, we have a character, Brooke, who's interesting to us because he's a character made up of contradictions. He's someone who likes to think he's a decent sort, but he also has this judgmental and moralistic side. I'm interested, as the story opens, to see what the consequences will be for him. I'm interested because he's what I call a dynamic character, "dynamic" in respect to being capable of motion in more than one direction. All it takes is the pairing of Brooke with Riley at a regional meeting of the Modern Language Association to provide the dramatic present for the working out of Brooke's character. That and a woman named Ruth, whom Brooke meets there.

The dramatic triangle of characters provides the means for Wolff's exploration of Brooke and how he comes up against the hard knowledge that the way he insists on seeing himself, this decent man, isn't the whole truth. His involvement with Ruth begins when he hurts her with an unintentional slight. She's prepared sandwiches for the conference, each of them having a literary quotation typed on a slip of paper attached to a toothpick stuck into the sandwich. Brooke, not aware that she's been the one to choose and type the quotes, tells her that they're "hard to swallow." When he sees that he's hurt her, he feels bad, and their journey begins, culminating in a night spent together, a fact that Riley, whom Brooke has always suspected of having affairs with his students, comes to note. At the end of the story Brooke, who has always sat in judgment of Riley, has now traded places with him. Brooke understands how we all have to kneel before one another.

If the story ended there, the epiphany would be too neat and not trustworthy. In our workshop yesterday we talked about why Wolff made the choice to extend the story, widening the point of view, to tell us that the chapter of his life that seemed to be closing for Brooke wasn't closing for others. Anonymous love poems appear in his mailbox at school. His wife, unpacking his bag after his trip to the MLA, smells perfume on his tie and his shirt. She fears the worst, but when Brooke comes home for dinner, he's so much like himself that she feels unworthy of him. The story ends with a reference to how the fearful feeling she has fades and becomes the sort of flutter that stops one cold from time to time and then goes away. There's a lesson here about how the end of a good story shouldn't be too neat, how it should close and open at the same time, and this is what Wolff accomplishes by letting the point of view widen after Brooke's neat observation that we all must kneel down before one another.

So, with Wolff's story as support, I suggested to my MFA students that the focus of our workshop this semester should be on deepening characters and situations and learning to think in terms of opposites. My objective would be to see if I could give them some shortcuts toward creating interesting, dynamic characters, allowing them to create their own troubles, and bringing the story to a moment of inevitable surprise, a moment in which something present from the beginning, but submerged, rises to the surface.

When we turned our attention to the stories from two of our own members, we spent time talking about how to complicate a main character's motive to give him or her that dynamic nature that Wolff gave Professor Brooke. The first story by one of the MFA students involved a complicated brother relationship and a dramatic situation that put pressure on that relationship. Our narrator, thinking that his married brother has had a sexual relationship with a girl that the narrator is sweet on, sets out to prove it. He tells himself he's doing so in order to protect the girl. What will make the narrator's motivation even more interesting will be to throw in another layer to his motive, one that's in opposition with his intent to be the decent man protecting the girl. If we can hint at the fact that the narrator resents his brother, we can establish the submerged thing that will rise by the end of the story, and that will be the narrator's desire not to prove his own decency but to prove his brother's indecency. This movement is suggested in the draft of the story, but we talked about pointing it up earlier.

Complicating the motive is a good lesson for us all to learn, and this writer's instincts had done just that. The key, it seems to me, to that inevitable surprise we're all wanting at the end of a story is to hit upon the contradictions within the main character relatively early in the narrative and to work with the story that the character tells himself about his motives versus an opposite layer that will rise because of the pressures of plot.

During our consideration of the second story from a member of the workshop, this issue of "tightening the screws" came up for discussion. Here I'm talking about letting a character's own actions in connection to the pressures from other characters or the pressures inherent in the dramatic situation make the main character squirm with uncertainty. In this particular story, which has a bit of magical realism blending with a very realistic style of telling, a young boy in long-ago England has an angel who it seems will leave him. The theory is that angels attach themselves to people who are virtuous and then leave them when that virtue is compromised. The story opens with a few pages of explanation of the situation, the characters, the setting, and it's all beautifully written. Then a few pages in we hit the complication. The family has always assumed the boy's angel will leave before the boy goes off to university, but that time has come, and the angel is still there. What will happen when the two of them are at university? That becomes the central question that tightens the screws on our main character. Sometimes a structural adjustment can help do that, putting pressure on the main character right away. I had a writing teacher once who said we should begin our stories as close to the end as possible. That strategy has the effect of putting immediate pressure on our main character. In the case of the story of the boy and his angel, I wonder what might happen if the story opened at university, if it opened, that is to say, in the midst of the dramatic present of the narrative. No need to lose the beautiful exposition from the opening. It can always be layered in after the dramatic present gives the story forward momentum.

So, when working to deepen a character or situation, keep in mind several key elements: urgency in the telling that comes from a writer connecting with the material in a profound way; contradictions within characters; dramatic irony; complicating a character's motive; preparing the way for the submerged layer to rise at the end; and putting pressure on the character (through structure and characterization) to make that submerged layer rise in a surprising and yet inevitable way.

Contradictory Characters

Our conversation in the fiction workshop began yesterday with a consideration of a chapter from Charles Baxter's excellent book *Burning Down the House*. The chapter "On Defamiliarization" deals with how writers can sometimes know their stories too early in the writing process. A writer might, for example, decide early on that his or her story is about the disruption of a family due to a father's alcoholism. Each scene, then, becomes one more example of the father's drinking and the ugly moments it causes for the family. As Baxter says, everything about the story fits. All of the arrows point in the same direction. He goes on to point out that in such cases the writers understand their characters too quickly, and therefore, the characters aren't contradictory or misfitted. "The truth that writers are after," Baxter says, "may be dramatic only if it has been forgotten first; if the story, in other words, pulls something contradictory and concealed out of its hiding place."

To help us think about how that magic trick happens in a good story, Baxter offers up the term *defamiliarization* from Russian formalist criticism and the Russian critic Viktor Shklovsky. Defamiliarization is the process by which the writer makes the familiar strange and the strange familiar. For me this boils down to the writer always being on the lookout for the unexpected that is also convincing and organic to the world of the story and its characters.

In Sherwood Anderson's "Adventure," from *Winesburg, Ohio*, a young woman named Alice Hindman constructs a narrative that she needs in order to believe in the future. The man she loves, Ned Currie, will come back to Winesburg from Chicago, as he's sworn he will, and they'll live happily ever after. But the years go on, and Ned doesn't return. At the end of the story, on a rainy night, Alice, so desperate for Ned Currie, so desperate for love, allows this despair, which is mixed up with eroticism, to overwhelm her. She strips off her clothes and runs out into the rain. She feels full of youth and courage. She sees a man stumbling around on the sidewalk ahead of her, and she makes a bold move. Anderson describes the moment with urgency and concision: "A wild, desperate mood took possession of her. 'What do I care who it is. He is alone, and I will go to him,' she thought; and then without stopping to consider the possible result of her madness, called softly. 'Wait!' she cried. 'Don't go away. Whoever you are, you must wait.'"

I'd like to pause here and consider Anderson at this point of the composition of the story, facing the choice of forming the man's response. What are some of the predictable options? The man reacts with shock? He reacts with lewdness, pleased by the sight of the woman and her nakedness? Either choice would fit nicely with what we expect, and for that reason each choice is flawed because it takes the story down a predictable path. It makes all the arrows point in the same direction. It fails to make the moment memorable. The story arrives somewhere familiar and, therefore, forgettable.

Now back to the story. The man, Alice notices, is an old man, perhaps somewhat deaf. He puts his hand to his mouth. He shouts. "What? What say?" Here we have a touch of what Baxter calls "surprising banality" to stand in contrast with Alice's brazen act and to throw it into bolder relief. Alice, noting the man's disregard of her nakedness—to him it doesn't matter a whit—recoils with shame. She runs back to her home and wonders whatever could have possessed her. She lies in bed and turns her face to the wall, accepting the loneliness that is now hers, a loneliness wrought because of the man's disregard. The story would never have reached this point if Anderson had followed a more predictable path with the man's reaction.

The lesson in this is that writers need to walk around their first ideas to see whether they've taken full advantage of the misfitted detail, image, or action. Providing a contrast between the familiar and the strange is often a way of drawing out that contradictory and concealed moment that's waiting at the end of a story. Ann Beattie once said that she wrote a story to a point where one of her characters said or did something unexpected and then another character said or did something equally unexpected. End of story. The key, of course, is to make sure that the unexpected is convincing given what we already know about the characters and their worlds. You can't just cue the ax murderer at the end of the story and call that a convincing surprise!

Odd Couples

The Writer as Matchmaker

We've been talking quite a bit in the fiction workshop about the necessity of a story arriving at a surprising and yet inevitable end. We've talked about how to build multidimensional characters by paying attention to their contradictory impulses and how to defamiliarize a character or a situation by allowing a misfit detail to arise. All of this asks us to keep an eye on the mysterious. By this I mean being on the lookout for the essence of a character or a situation that is in some way unsayable and, therefore, in need of the story to dramatize its energy.

To that end we stayed with Charles Baxter's *Burning Down the House* yesterday and looked at a chapter called "Counterpointed Characterization." In this chapter Baxter takes to task the conflict model for the structure of a short story. That is to say, the protagonist pitted against an antagonist; one person wants something, and another person wants something else. *Voilà.* Conflict. Baxter argues that stories often don't work that way. He says that conflict can actually be very slight in a short story and that often counterpointed characterization creates the tension.

By counterpointed characterization he means the pairing of characters who "bring out a crucial response to each other." When that happens, Baxter says, "a latent energy rises to the surface, the desire or secret previously forced down into psychic obscurity." Therefore, Baxter argues, instead of asking the question connected to the conflict model story ("Will the protagonist get what he or she wants?"), the more appropriate question for a story that depends upon counterpointed characterization for its tension is "What's emerging here?" To this I'll add that our interest in characters and their situations in a well-crafted story almost always comes from wondering what aspect of character or situation will show up at the end of the story, having worked its way up through whatever denial or facade the character has constructed, to be that additional element of truth, surprising and yet inevitable, that gives the end of a good story its resonance.

In Alice Walker's "Everyday Use" two sisters share center stage. Maggie, the slow-witted but lovable sister, lives at home with her mother, who narrates the story. As our narrative opens, Maggie and her mother are awaiting the arrival of Dee, the beautiful, articulate, and upwardly mobile sister. The two sisters are all wrong for each other, and for that reason they make a good pairing for the tension of the story. Notice, though, that they aren't complete polar opposites. Although very much different, they're still of the same blood, and they recall the same ancestors, family customs, and such. As Baxter points out, a short story writer has to be a good matchmaker, and if the match is too simple, the resulting story will be too. Therefore, it's good to pair characters who, though different, also have some common ground. Think of Felix and Oscar in Neil Simon's play *The Odd Couple*. A neat freak and a slob. Polar opposites. The stuff of comedy in this case. But Oscar is a divorced man, separated from his ex and their children. Felix is living outside his home, fearing that he's on the verge of becoming an ex-husband. He and Oscar, then, share the loneliness and regret of men who no longer have their families, and that's what deepens their characters and their situations, and the gravity of their loneliness works its way up throughout the course of the play.

In "Everyday Use" Alice Walker gets similar mileage from the pairing of Maggie and Dee and a mother who must make a choice. Dee, upon arriving for her visit, asks for some of the family quilts. She'll hang them on her walls, she says, pointing out that if Maggie gets them, she'll put them to everyday use and wear them out. So, we have the right pairing of dissimilar characters within the same family and the tension that results over the request for the quilts and the mother's decision to give them to Maggie. The character who we imagined might be overlooked is the one who rises to the top by the end of the story, by virtue of her goodness and her appreciation and knowledge of family history. The more intelligent, more glamorous, more successful Dee is left out in the cold.

Think of any story that you admire and see if the appropriate counterpointed characterization makes possible the interest that you have in that story. In our workshop yesterday, thanks to Baxter's thoughts and his examples from "Everyday Use," "The Misfit," and "The Dead," we kicked around ideas for how a third character in the student stories we discussed could be put to use as the catalyst to whatever shifts between the two main characters.

Often in a good story a character maintains a certain idea of him- or herself, and this character finds him- or herself acting from behind that facade while interacting with another main character. The entrance of a third character can cause the facade to crumble. Emerging, then, is the truth of the character that he or she's either not been aware of or has been trying to conceal. Think of Michael Furey in James Joyce's "The Dead" and how his evocation at the end of that story causes everything to shift for Gabriel and his wife, Gretta. Gretta's story of how Michael, years ago, stood in the rain to profess his love for her and then died soon after makes it impossible for Gabriel to maintain the facade he's constructed for himself. The passion in that story points out how much Gabriel is lacking the same. He'll never be able to think of himself in quite the same way.

The lesson in all of this is the interesting dynamic that results when the right pairing of characters exerts pressure until some-thing emerges that wouldn't otherwise. It's that "something" that usually gives a good story its resonance.

Characterization in the Personal Essay

Our conversation in workshop today centered on Phillip Lopate's craft article "Writing Personal Essays: On the Necessity of Turning Oneself into a Character," which appears in *Writing Creative Nonfiction*, edited by Carolyn Forché and Philip Gerard. Lopate points out the importance of the essayist becoming a round character in his or her essay, dramatizing the writer's complexities and tapping into what Lopate calls "teeming inner lives." Lopate suggests cutting away the inessentials of our characters and highlighting those features that lead to contradictions or ambivalence.

Characters become interesting to us when they act against type, giving us something we didn't expect. If we provide a baseline of the character by establishing a pattern of habits and actions, then any variation that hits upon another aspect of the personality will immediately resonate with readers. As Lopate points out, the personal essayist needs to take an inventory of his or her idiosyncrasies, inconsistencies, and quirks. He also stresses the importance of being able to view oneself from some distance and with a degree of self-amusement while also being willing to analyzing the flaws in one's thinking. All of this is necessary to seeing oneself in the round, thereby becoming a vibrant and interesting character in your own essay.

But how does one do that? one of my MFA students asked. How does one go about dramatizing the self from a position of contradiction or ambivalence? It's a fair question of what means best produce the desired result. It's a question that perhaps I can begin to answer with a writing activity. I'll admit that I haven't thought this one all the way through yet, but I'm sort of circling the center the way a good personal essayist approaches his or her material, viewing it from this angle and that, trying to see as fully as possible, paying attention to leaps in thought, associations of images, juxtapositions of scenes. So, feel free to take these prompts and turn them however you'd like. We'll consider them suggestions that when put into some sort of order will allow you to practice some strategies for turning yourself into an interesting character in your essays.

1. Start with a moment of regret, perhaps one that still strikes a note of ambivalence in you or otherwise locates itself with the contradictions of your own character. Perhaps you've created this moment of regret via your own actions or words. Lopate talks about the importance of giving yourself something to do in the essay, an action that creates certain consequences. Brenda Miller's essay "Swerve" (*Brevity*, issue 31), for example, begins with our author running over a piece of wood in the road: "I'm sorry about that time I ran over a piece of wood in the road. A pound of marijuana in the trunk and a faulty brake light—any minute the cops might have pulled us over, so you were edgy already, and then I ran over that piece of stray lumber without even slowing down." For the purpose of this prompt, you might begin with, "I'm sorry . . ." or "I regret that I . . ." or "If I could, I'd . . ." The objective is to begin to create the character you were in a specific moment from the past, one that still haunts you, fills you with shame, makes you feel like apologizing.

2. Take a step back, speaking now from your adult perspective, about the younger character you've begun to create for yourself. Establish a baseline for that younger self. You might begin, "When I was twelve, it was my habit to . . ."

3. Now introduce a variation: "But one day, I . . ."

4. Who were you at the time you're recalling? Consider the communities in which you had membership—your family, your church, your grade school class. You might begin with "I was . . ." Gee, just tell us who you were, concen-

trating on offering only what we need to know about your character to highlight the contradictions or ambivalence relevant to the moment of regret you're recalling.

5. Complicate your character. You might fill in the following line: "At times I . . . , but there were also times when I . . ."
6. Look at yourself from a distance, perhaps with self-amusement. You might begin with "Who was that boy [or girl] who . . ."
7. Analyze your own flaws. You might begin with "Maybe I was wrong to . . . , but . . ."
8. End with a confession: "I confess that I . . ." or "What I never told anyone was that . . ."

It's my hope that these prompts, in whatever order and form you choose to use them, will help you feel your own character deepening as you revisit a moment of regret. In the process you should feel what you can do with perspective, persona, modulation of voice, and the variations of your own personality (the inconsistencies and quirks and flaws) that make you a memorable and multidimensional character as displayed through action and through the adult narrator's perspective on the person he or she was.

It was interesting to me that our conversation about one of the student-written essays today focused upon a structural rearrangement that took away the question of whether a childhood friendship would endure. Letting the readers know early on that the friendship would unravel demanded that we replace that tension with a new one, the question of how two girls, raised in the same place and with similar interests, could take such different paths in life.

The question "Why?" is often more interesting than the question "What?" Character is always more compelling than plot, although plots can of course be foremost if created by the character that the writer is making of him- or herself on the page. Lopate talks about the importance of conflict in personal essays:

"What gives an essay dynamism is the need to work out some problem, especially a problem that is not easily resolved." So, we create ourselves as characters in our essays, people who are conflicted and trying to reach some sort of balance. We have to be able to see ourselves as clearly and with as much insight as we do the characters we create of others.

Creating Richer Characters

Last week in workshop we talked about turning oneself into a character in creative nonfiction. This week our focus was on creating compelling characters of other people. My students read a roundtable consideration on this craft issue that was published in a long-ago issue of *Fourth Genre*. One of the participants, Donald Morrill, talks about how characters in nonfiction "don't exist just for our purposes—because they live." In other words, unlike in fiction, where characters are invented by whatever means necessary, the characters who populate our nonfiction are real people who live or have lived. Morrill goes on to say that what fascinates us about these nonfiction characters is the part of them that lies out of sight. "Most of life is a secret kept by banality," Morrill says. I love this line because it's so true, and it's so much at the center of how we go about creating characters of real people on the page.

Just like when we write fiction, our nonfiction characters should be capable of surprising us. We shouldn't be fitting them to a specific mold of the type of person we determine them to be; we should allow them the free will to be someone outside of type. We should be alert for those words and actions that provide an additional layer to their characters (a layer surprising and yet accurate) and thereby surprise us with what we've come to know. We should make our nonfiction characters as round and multi-dimensional as any unforgettable character in a work of fiction.

I'm mulling over something else that Morrill says: "Character in nonfiction is shaped as much by an author's omissions as by action." If our secret lives are hidden by banality, does a reader's awareness of that fact lead him or her to believe that there's always something more interesting just below the surface of any person or, more to our focus, below the surface of nonfiction characters? Are the beneficial omissions that Morrill references the aspects of people's characters that are at first submerged, hidden behind the banal details, but that rise to the top via the skillful hand of the nonfiction writer interested in making characters vibrant for us by peeling away layers of the commonplace to finally hit upon the aspects of the genuine, the parts of people they usually prefer to keep hidden? To me the omissions aren't really omissions. They exist as soon as the nonfiction character steps onto the page. They're just camouflaged. I consider it my job to strip the camouflage away by finding the moment in which this person became someone different to me, someone fuller, richer, more complex.

To help with that, here's a writing activity that should help you practice seeing more in people than may at first be apparent, a necessary step toward creating more interesting characters in your nonfiction:

1. Choose someone you've shared space and time with—a parent, a sibling, an aunt or uncle, a grandparent, a friend, a boss—you fill in the blank. Make sure this someone is a person whom you want to understand better. Then choose a particular prop for that person, something specific that you associate with them: a brown fedora, a Scripto mechanical pencil, an embroidered handkerchief. Find some detail that begins to make this person come alive to you.

2. Close your eyes and remember a specific time when you saw this person holding his or her prop. I'll give you some memory prompts to help you recall sensory details associated with that moment. Observe the scene, making a movie in your mind. What do you see? Allow your other senses to participate. What do you hear? Perhaps you recall specific lines of dialogue. What do you taste? Smell? Feel? What kind of day is it? What's the one thing

you'd like to ask this person but can't? If you did work up the nerve to pose the question, how do you think this person would respond? When these details are vivid in your mind, open your eyes and start jotting down everything that has stayed with you: the details, the dialogue, the questions.

3. Recall a time that your character's interaction with his or her prop led to the revelation of another aspect of that person's character, one that surprised you. Using a limited number of sentences—let's say between five and ten, so you'll be sure to make every word count, every sentence precise—present a vivid and multidimensional portrait of this person. Use more than one of the senses. Allow the details to bring out the depth of your subject, simultaneously creating an intimacy with this person as well as evoking the feeling that there's still more for you and us to know about him or her.

4. To what questions does your portrait lead you? What do you want to know about your subject? Answer the questions by beginning to freewrite with the words "I imagine . . ." or "I wonder whether . . . ." Try to imagine the inner life of this person more deeply than you have previously. Don't be afraid of the questions you don't know how to answer; let the details lead you to explorations of those questions.

It's interesting to think about how the specific detail can simultaneously lead us to the vivid and the mysterious. How can something known lead to something unknown? What does this say about the resonance of any particular detail—about its reliability or perhaps its error? As writers, we're taught to trust in the specific, to rely on the things of the world to carry emotional and psychological significance, and yet it seems that the precise detail can open a world or a life in a way that illuminates while also pointing toward darkness that the writer must try to navigate.

That's all to the good because it requires further writing, and in the process, if we're open to the exploration—if we'll only follow the details—we'll discover more of the truth of a situation or a character than we perhaps knew existed. All because we trusted in the details and how they can illuminate while also challenging us to uncover more.

The Art of the Snark

Is it just me, or is it true that somewhere along the line we became a culture that values (nay, practically demands) the snark? You know what I'm talking about, that sharp-tongued voice that cuts to the quick, that often mean-spirited comment meant to belittle. We hear it on our television shows and in our movies, in our dinner table conversations, in our classrooms, in much of the fiction that we read.

As summer settles in and I have a chance to do a good deal of reading, I'm noticing the degree of sarcasm that some novelists give their characters—usually young, hip characters who think they have something smart to say about the world around them. It's not that I'm totally against the snark; a zinger of a line can be refreshing. What was it Dorothy Parker said? "If all the girls who attended the Yale prom were laid end to end, I wouldn't be a bit surprised." And Cole Porter? "He may have hair upon his chest but, sister, so has Lassie." But let's not forget Noel Coward, who said, "Wit ought to be a glorious treat like caviar; never spread it about like marmalade." Too much snark, as Coward makes plain, piles up and gets sluggish and starts to become annoying.

Which leads me to that classic snark, Holden Caulfield from *The Catcher in the Rye*. In a scene early in the novel, Holden is trying to read a book but keeps getting interrupted by another student, Ackley. Ackley asks him if the book is any good, and Holden says, "This *sentence* I'm reading is terrific." Holden then admits that he can be very sarcastic when he wants to be. And yet the same Holden is capable of compassion, sometimes even toward those whom he derides. He is, most memorably, a person who fantasizes that he's the protector of children. He tells his sister:

Anyway, I keep picturing all these little kids playing some game in this big field of rye and all. Thousands of little kids, and nobody's around—nobody big, I mean—except me. And I'm standing on the edge of some crazy cliff. What I have to do, I have to catch everybody if they start to go over the cliff—I mean if they're running and they don't look where they're going. I have to come out from somewhere and *catch* them. That's all I'd do all day. I'd just be the catcher in the rye and all. I know it's crazy, but that's the only thing I'd really like to be. I know it's crazy.

For all his sarcasm, all his cynicism, all his distrust of phony people, he's genuinely worried about his little sister and by extension "thousands of little kids," whom he wants to save. His compassion exists beneath the facade of his snark; the pressures of the plot make that facade crack from time to time, and the kinder, more genuine Holden is visible. The snark can't hold, as it does in too many novels and stories these days. The sharp word, the sarcastic attitude, the cynical eye? Life has a way of breaking down the confidence it takes to put those tools to work, at least temporarily, if not forever. A good fiction writer knows that. A good novelist is interested in the aspect of a character that's hidden—the fear, perhaps, or the insecurity—that makes the construction of that snarky facade necessary and at the same time impossible to maintain.

PART 3 ❧ Detail

A House of Straw, a House of Sticks,
a House of Bricks

The truth of the story lies in the details.

—PAUL AUSTER

My Mother Gives Me a Writing Lesson

Today I'm reading through some old letters from my mother, written in her widowhood, and I'm struck by the sound of my own voice in hers and the lesson she offers the writer I'll one day be about how to let the details evoke a life: "The little garden I have planted just stands there. No potatoes ever came up. I don't know if it will grow when it warms up or not. If it does we might have some spinach or lettuce when you come home. But I can't promise any. I've been using onions from those I set out last fall. I want to get some cabbage and cauliflower as soon as the stores get their plants." Flannery O'Connor, in *Mysteries and Manners*, talks about how the meaning of a story has to be made concrete through the details. "Detail has to be controlled by some overall purpose," she says, "and every detail has to work for you." She goes on to suggest that these details be gathered from "the texture of the existence" that forms the world of the story. "You can't cut characters off from their society and say much about them as individuals," she says. "You can't say anything meaningful about the mystery of a personality unless you put that personality in a believable and significant social context."

My mother wrote this letter to me while I was in the MFA program at the University of Arkansas in Fayetteville. A ten-hour drive separated me from her home, a home I'd had to leave her in alone because, two weeks before the move to Fayetteville, my father died. My mother was seventy-two at the time, and she hadn't had a driver's license for some time. To leave her was, at that time of my life, the hardest thing I'd ever done.

Now, as I read this passage from her letter, I find the essence of her life in those days rising from the details that she includes: the garden where the potatoes have refused to come up, the hope for spinach or lettuce when I return, the acknowledgment that she shouldn't hope for too much, but still the dream of cabbage and cauliflower plants to come. Each detail expressing some aspect of what it was to be her at that time in her life, each detail holding the person she was in that place. If I encountered this passage in a story, I'd love the writer's trust in the details, and I'd love how they so simply and yet elegantly create the meaning of this character's life.

We fiction writers have to pay attention to the worlds of our characters and to the way the objects of those worlds become expressive. So, with that in mind, here's a writing exercise:

1. Gather the details of the setting of a story that you're working on, or one that you've completed, to which you want to add more cultural texture. Pay attention to sensory details, not limiting yourself to the visual. What are the sounds of this place? The smells? The textures? The tastes? What are the customs?

2. Zero in on the details that are intimately connected to your main character. What do they show you about him or her that you didn't know? What do they confirm about your character that you already thought you knew? Are the details, for example, expressive of certain cultural attitudes? Is your main character acting in accordance with the cultural influences of the setting, or is he or she acting in resistance to those attitudes?

3. Have your main character engage in an activity that is common in this culture—playing music for tips in the subway, for example, or planting flowers in the garden or attending the symphony or bingo night at the American Legion. Or have your character do something that would be considered out of place in this culture. The key is to have your character act from his or her relationship with the culture in which he or she lives.

4. Find a place within the scene to rely solely on details, à la

the passage from my mother's lesson, to express something essential, but something impossible to say directly, about your character's life.

Our characters come from specific worlds. Whether by birthright or adoption, fiction writers cozy up to particular landscapes and use them to give their writing authority, contribute to characterization, suggest plots, and influence tone and atmosphere. The details of a place can create the characters and their actions.

Get the Particulars Right

One of my favorite books is Flannery O'Connor's *Mystery and Manners.* In the section "The Nature and Aim of Fiction" she spends some time reminding us that fiction is concrete: "The beginning of human knowledge is through the senses, and the fiction writer begins where human perception begins. He appeals through the senses, and you cannot appeal to the senses with abstractions." The important thing for us to note here is that fiction creates a convincing world through its particulars. Slight the reader on sensory details, and it's tough for the world of the story or the novel to seem real. If the world doesn't convince, then it's likely that the characters and their actions and thoughts won't either. So much of the work of fiction is done on the seemingly small scale of what things look like, smell like, sound like, taste like, feel like. The blending of two or three sensory details (isn't it funny how often three is the magic number in fiction?) in a scene immediately creates a vivid world that the reader will have a hard time denying. Instead, that reader will be immersed in that very specific world.

O'Connor quotes a brief passage from Flaubert's *Madame Bovary* as an example. Charles Bovary is watching Emma at the piano: "She struck the notes with aplomb and ran from top to bottom of the keyboard without a break. Thus shaken up, the old instrument, whose strings buzzed, could be heard at the other end of the village when the window was open, and often the bailiff's clerk, passing along the highroad, bareheaded and in list slippers, stopped to listen, his sheet of paper in his hand." Notice the level of concreteness in this passage: the way Emma plays the piano, the buzzing of the strings traveling to the other end of the village through an open window and to the ears of

88

the bailiff's clerk, who is bareheaded and wearing list slippers. He stops to listen, a sheet of paper in his hands. As O'Connor points out, Flaubert had to create a believable village in which to put Emma. Before she could exist, the village had to exist. For her actions to be convincing, they had to happen in a vivid and specific place. O'Connor says, "It's always necessary to remember that the fiction writer is much less immediately concerned with grand ideas and bristling emotions than he is with putting list slippers on clerks." Get the particulars right, and they will contain "grand ideas" and "bristling emotions."

O'Connor also makes us aware that fiction is presented rather than reported. A piece of fiction is "a self-contained dramatic unit" that carries its meaning inside it. She says, "You can't make an inadequate dramatic action complete by putting a statement of meaning on the end of it or in the middle of it or at the beginning of it. . . . when you write fiction you are speaking *with* character and action, not *about* character and action." This is what we mean when we say that a good writer creates his or her characters from the inside. In other words, through the concrete particulars and the way a character responds to them, a writer inhabits that character, taking him or her through a series of meaningful events.

I'm interested in how a writer allows the meaning to lift up from the particulars of a piece of fiction without comment on the writer's part. O'Connor says the vision of the writer invites us to investigate how the proper arrangement of characters and events can convey the significance and the resonance of a piece of fiction. Anagogical vision, she says, allows us "to see different levels of reality in one image or one situation." I'd like to add the word *character* to that situation, inviting us to think about how interesting characters are made up of contradictions, in a sense holding different levels of reality simultaneously. O'Connor allows us to think about this as a matter of the writer's vision. In other words, how capable are we, as writers, to see what exists simultaneously within a character, a situation, a detail, an image?

O'Connor talks about the importance of having a way of reading the world and its people that includes the most possibilities, and she says: "I think it is this enlarged view of the human scene that the fiction writer has to cultivate if he is ever going to write stories that have any chance of becoming a permanent part of our literature. It seems to be a paradox that the larger and more complex the personal view, the easier it is to compress it into fiction."

So, how do we begin to develop our anagogical vision? I've always thought that it begins by putting it into practice in our personal lives, but I'll leave you to think about how that works or doesn't for you. I know that as a writer, we live among our characters in these convincing worlds that we create. We get inside a character's skin, and we experience the world the way he or she experiences it. Does the way a character chooses to see herself and the world around her have a good deal to do with the vision that the writer has of the world around him or her? My instinct tells me to say, yes. We can take the basic premise of any piece of fiction, give it to five different writers, and likely get five unique stories that use the same events. In other words, those events will contain different meanings, each dependent on the vision of the individual writer. But to answer my question about how we develop our anagogical vision when we're writing, let me suggest that we challenge ourselves to think in terms of opposites.

Take, for example, the chain of events from this story. The main character comes out of a confrontation scene with a homeless family, a slightly different man than he was when he entered it. When he goes to his ex-wife's house to tell her the story, he's a man who wants to deny that he stole a backpack that held the money the family had and then threw it into the deep woods, where they'll have a hard time finding it. He wants to pretend he had every right to do that because the family has no business squatting in the woods of the park. He wants above all to forget that the family exists. So, he enters this final scene passing judgment. Using this as a test case for how thinking in terms of opposites can pay off for a writer, I'd say we're at a make-or-break point for this story. So much depends on what lifts up from this final scene. It seems to me that the resonance will come from our ability to hold opposing ideas in our heads simultaneously. If we ask ourselves what the opposite of judgment is, I suppose we'd say compassion or forgiveness. The arrangement of the story has brought us to this point, where, if we choose, the door can stand wide open, making room for what's on either side of it: judgment, forgiveness. Let's say our main character divorced his wife because she was a hoarder and that fact contributed to the marriage's ruin. Isn't this the common ground that the man has with the family in the woods, who have obviously come to some degree of ruin themselves? When he stands outside his ex-wife's home, which used to be his home too, and sees the physical clutter and ruin of that house, isn't he ready to enlarge his vision of the world, to dismantle the facade of judgment behind which he's been operating, behind which waits the rising compassion for imperfect lives? Can't that judgment and that forgiveness coexist in a moment that contains the meaning of the story? Please note that the final move of the story can't execute a 180-degree turn for the character, shifting from pure judgment to pure compassion. That's too simple and not convincing at all because it doesn't hold enough layers of truth. There's the benefit of thinking in opposites, getting at that rich layer of meaning. Remember what O'Connor says: "The larger and more complex the personal view, the easier it is to compress it into fiction."

So, create a convincing world through sensory details, move your characters through a meaningful sequence of events within that world, and practice enlarging your personal vision so you can think it terms of opposites. Be on the lookout for that aspect of the story that you may not have known was rising but was actually there from the very beginning. All you have to do is adjust your vision to look for it.

Know Your Place

American rocker John Mellencamp calls Bloomington, Indiana, home. Bloomington is what we'd call a hop, skip, and a jump from where I grew up, just over the state line in the agricultural land of southeastern Illinois.

Mellencamp, in his 1985 song "Small Town," has a line that ends with a preposition, a line about the places from which we come. It's clunky, but because we're practically neighbors (because we share the landscape of the rural Midwest), I forgive him. Whether by birthright or adoption, fiction writers cozy up to particular landscapes and use them to give their writing authority, contribute to characterization, suggest plots, and influence tone and atmosphere.

Ann Beattie's book *Mrs. Nixon* is part portrait of Pat Nixon and part exploration of the fiction writer's art. In one passage Beattie talks about how fiction writers can claim specific territories: "In writing fiction convincingly, what they [the writers] have to do is point to a specific literary sky, a sky under which anything is possible, and move their characters through a landscape that's right for them, even though their scribes may live elsewhere, or prefer other territory."

In our MFA workshop yesterday we considered three student-written stories, and each of them made good use of the individual writer's "literary sky." That is to say, each story came from a very specific world that each writer knew intimately. Consequently, the characters created their own plots from the particulars of their very specific landscapes. A story of infidelity and romantic disillusionment in India, an indoctrination into the difficulty of knowing in the face of evil in rural Kentucky, an act of violent retribution bred from small-town culture in West Virginia. Each story and its characters were so connected to their particular landscapes that their actions were utterly convincing. For the fiction writer that's the first battle. If we are precise about our settings, our characters and their choices will ring with authority.

What will I remember from these three stories long into the future? The American woman in India who, while traveling in a car with her married lover, glances out the window and sees a man riding a bicycle, a pyramid of eggs strapped to the back fender. That detail, so anchored in the landscape, becomes an image for the heart of the story, holding, as it does, everything that is lovely and fragile about the relationship between the woman and her lover. First and foremost, though, it's a detail that comes from the writer's intimate knowledge of his literary sky.

I'll also remember the description of the forest sounds in the Kentucky night when a young boy, eager to prove his manhood, waits in his father's truck, keeping watch over a sleeping man who's about to wake and take the boy down a path that will shake him and challenge the way he's always known his father and himself. The sound of a barred owl's monkey screech coming from the forest speaks volumes about where this scene is heading. It's a detail organic to the world of the story, and it's one that helps create an atmosphere necessary to the scene unfolding.

Finally, I'll remember the achingly beautiful scene of an absent-from-the-family father cutting his daughter's hair on a riverbank in West Virginia and how the hair falls onto the grass and the father snatches up a bit of it and puts it in his pocket. The world is so real to me because it's so intimately known by the writer. Later, when this same father finds himself in a precarious position, kidnapped and waiting in a cave for his executioner, I'm persuaded because I've seen the act itself come from the choices of characters in response to the world they occupy, a world of drug abuse, machismo, and corruption.

Landscape in fiction is both a conductor and a receiver. It can both create and express the actions and emotions of a story, but first it has to be there in all its intimate particulars. Consider,

as but one example, the end of James Joyce's story "The Dead."
Gabriel listens to his wife's story of the frail, ill Michael Furey,
a boy who loved her so deeply he left his sickbed and went out
into the rainy night in hopes that he might persuade her to come
downstairs from her grandmother's house and be with him one
more time before she went away in the morning to the convent.
Gretta sobs with the sad remembrance of how she told Michael
to go home lest he "get his death in the rain" and how he told
her "he did not want to live." Gabriel must confront the truth of
Michael Furey's great love for Gretta and the romance she once
felt: "He [Gabriel] had never felt like that himself towards any
woman but he knew that such a feeling must be love." Gabriel's
own feeling of self-importance shrivels at the end of the story,
and in addition to his knowledge of the romance between Gretta
and Michael, he also accepts the mortality that is the truth of
all their lives: "One by one they were all becoming shades." The
very last move of the story features the landscape, and Joyce's
description illustrates how that landscape holds the emotions
that Gabriel can't express to Gretta. From their bedroom window he watches the snow falling outside:

> Yes, the newspapers were right: snow was general all over
> Ireland. It was falling on every part of the dark, central plain,
> on the treeless hills, falling softly upon the Bog of Allen and,
> farther westward, softly falling into the dark mutinous Shan-
> non waves. It was falling, too, upon every part of the lonely
> churchyard on the hill where Michael Furey lay buried. It lay
> thickly drifted on the crooked crosses and headstones, on
> the spears of the little gate, on the barren thorns. His soul
> swooned slowly as he heard the snow falling faintly through
> the universe and faintly falling, like the descent of their last
> end, upon all the living and the dead.

The smallness that Gabriel now feels, the diminished self-
importance, is projected out onto the landscape, particularly

the churchyard where Michael Furey is buried, where everything is being covered with snow.

If writers know their places fully, they'll not only paint a convincing portrait of the setting; they'll also understand how landscape becomes necessary to the characters, their stories, their emotions, and to everything the writer has come to the page to explore.

I'll close by suggesting a writing exercise:

Identify one of your "literary skies," a place you know intimately. What are the particulars of that place? Don't neglect the sensory details. Think about the customs and cultural attitudes of that place. Are the people similar to the landscape? What do they do or say that connects them with the place where they live? Or perhaps they exist in opposition to the setting. Perhaps they resist its particulars and its culture. Create a single character. Write an opening scene in which you portray the setting and have this character perform an action that's either a result of his or her connection to the place or else is in opposition to it. See where that single act, bred from landscape, can take the character down a chain of causally connected events.

That Kind of Place

An Argument for Nostalgia

Why is it, once you reach a certain age, that Sundays are loaded with nostalgia? Today I'm thinking of summer Sundays when I lived on our farm in southeastern Illinois. I'm talking about an eighty-acre plot of land on the Lawrence County side of the County Line Road. Eighty acres of clay soil in Lukin Township that my father planted in wheat, soybeans, and corn. The roads ran at right angles, mostly in straight lines. The fences did the same. A lane ran east from the County Line Road and led to our farmhouse on top of a gentle rise shaded by two maple trees and a giant oak.

I was the only child of older parents, my mother being forty-five and my father forty-one when I was born. As many of you know, he lost both of his hands in a corn picker when I was barely a year old. He was fitted with prostheses, and he continued to farm. My mother, who was a grade school teacher, helped him when she could. I had friends who lived on the next farm to our north, and we played together, but I spent a good deal of time on my own, entertaining myself.

An oak tree stood beside our mailbox at the end of the lane. So many days I stood in the front yard of our home and looked down the lane toward that tree, hoping beyond hope that I'd see a cloud of dust rising up from the road, a sign of a car coming, and I'd hope that car would slow and turn into our lane and come to pay a visit because out there in the country, particularly on those hot days when summer had nearly worn you down, you could get anxious for a change of pace, and a little company, particularly if that meant other kids to play with, was just the ticket.

The flat land sectioned off into blocks of fields, the roads running straight and squared, a tree like this to shade the mouth of a lane that led to a house where on Sundays, after a week of hard work, people were at rest. When I was a boy, this was my tribe: my mother and father and the aunts and uncles and cousins who came to visit after church services were done. They came bringing angel food cakes and Jell-O salads and sugar pies and hot dishes of baked beans and chicken and noodles and cold ones of potato salad and slaw, and we sat down around the table to eat. My childhood was so often a time of hoping that someone might come to call, someone who would break through the fenced-in squares of land and jumble things up a tad. I could even get excited when our cows sometimes got loose, somehow got beyond the barbed wire, and ended up in our yard or out on the County Line Road or over in some other farmer's pasture. I loved the fact that the ordinary all of a sudden seemed strange. Seeing a Jersey cow by my rope swing that hung from the maple tree in front of our house? Now that was something outside the regular come and go.

My father must have sometimes felt that same desire to break free. One Sunday, toward evening, when it was nearing time for all the company to pack up and leave, he said he bet he could beat me in a race. I must have been six or seven at the time, which means he would have been forty-seven or forty-eight. The numbers of his age meant nothing to me at the time, but I was always aware that he and my mother were much older than the parents of my friends, and of course, I'd learned the stares people gave my father's prosthetic hands. I knew that he was an oddity.

Which may explain why he challenged me to that race. Maybe he was tired of the role he'd been cast into because of his accident. Maybe he felt the freedom of a Sunday afternoon dwindling down with evening chores soon to come and then another week of work in the fields. Maybe he wanted, at least for a brief time, to be free of all of that. A race. Something he could do with his legs. Something he could do with his son just the way other, younger fathers did.

I was delighted. It was perhaps the first time my father had seemed like other fathers to me. We raced across the yard. I laughed as I ran. My father lumbered past me, and I laughed to see him run. Then, at the finish line, he slipped. His feet went out from under him, and he fell on his back, embarrassed, hurt, and I stopped and watched while my uncles helped him up, and I felt an ache in my throat because I'd caused all of that to happen just by being alive.

Often these days I wonder whether young writers know their own tribes well enough. We should all pay attention to our communities, our landscapes, so we can see how our characters act from either their sense of belonging or a resistance to the geography and the culture. We need to understand that our people and the places they occupy are never separate. We need the sort of intimate knowledge of people and places that the nostalgic impulse can bring.

When I was a boy, I lived in the kind of place where a man could try to escape all that yoked him to the land and to the limitations of his own body, the kind of place where his son could feel ashamed for coming to his parents so late in their lives. My mother and father and I and all the people around us—we lived in a place like that.

Nostalgia and the Memoirist

The issue of nostalgia in memoir came up once in one of my MFA workshops, and we explored the question of how a memoirist can deal in nostalgia without becoming nostalgic. Hmm . . . that may at first sound like a goofy question to chase around the workshop table, but please bear with me.

The word *nostalgia* has its roots in the Ancient Greek word for "a return home." We define it now as a longing for home or familiar surroundings; a homesickness; a yearning for things of the past.

At the risk of stating the obvious, all writers of memoir deal with the things of the past; all memoirists, then, are in some way returning "home." This journey carries with it a certain degree of risk. Memoir goes sour quickly, its falseness showing through, once it's clear that the writer's impulse is to celebrate, to romanticize, to indulge in sentimentality.

Such is sometimes the case in the dreams I often have of the farm in southeastern Illinois where I spent my early years with my mother and father. In those dreams the house, which is now in ruins, has been rebuilt. My parents' youth and health have been restored. The grass is green, the birds are singing, and happiness reigns. You get the idea: everything is peachy keen. But that's only one part of the lives we all lived in that farmhouse; my dreams conveniently edit out the struggles, the yearning, the anger, the suffering, the embarrassment of people who loved one another but who often fell short of that love. Apparently, there's no room in my dreams for those truths. Maybe that's because I've made a place for them in the memoirs I've written.

To deal in nostalgia without becoming nostalgic, a writer has to be honest, has to see the entire palette of the experience, both the bright colors and the dark ones. As is the case with almost any craft issue connected to a piece of writing, help comes in the form of this question: what was the impulse that first brought the writer to the page? In memoir that impulse can't be a nostalgic one, can't come from an intention to romanticize; a memoirist's intention must be to see the self and the other people in his or her world with a clear eye, one meant for the honest exploration of the multiple layers of human experience.

Which brings me to Ted Kooser's essay "Small Rooms in Time." This is an essay about a murder that takes place in a house where Kooser and his family lived before the divorce that sent them in different directions. Kooser says of the murder: "It's taken me a long time to try to set down my feelings about this incident. At the time, it felt as if somebody had punched me in the stomach, and in ways it has taken me until now to get my breath back. I'm ashamed to say that it wasn't the boy's death that so disturbed me, but the fact that it happened in a place where my family and I had once been safe." Notice how the essay bravely wades into nostalgia ("a place where my family and I had once been safe"), but it does so with a point of emphasis on uncomfortable honesty ("I'm ashamed to say that it wasn't the boy's death that so disturbed me"), thereby signaling the unflinching eye that will guide us through this return home.

At one point in the essay Kooser talks about how the house, after the murder, became permanently clear to him: "Since the murder I have often peered into those little rooms where things went good for us at times and bad at times. I have looked into the miniature house and seen us there as a young couple, coming and going, carrying groceries in and out, hats on, hats off, happy and sad." It's the honest admission of the bad times in concert with the good, the sad with the happy, that earns Kooser the right to remember in loving detail the facts of the life he lived in that house; it allows him to deal in nostalgia without becoming nostalgic. His intention isn't to romanticize but to deal honestly with the circumstances and the effect, years later, that the murder has wrought on his memory of the past and his notion of himself in the present. Because he admits the sometimes unhappiness of his young family, we believe what he says thereafter. Of the house he says: "The murder brought it forward and made me hold it under the light again. Of course I hadn't really forgotten, nor could I ever forget how it feels to be a young father, frightened by an enormous and threatening world, wondering what might become of him, what might become of his wife and son."

The lesson for those of us who write memoir? Admit it all, every aspect of whatever home we're revisiting, and then state the details, present the objects that furnished our rooms, simply and plainly without commentary. The resonance of the rugs, the sofas, the paintings, the draperies, the empty chairs, will come from the fact that we attach nothing to them except the truth that we were, even in that place and time, imperfect.

A Detail and All It Can Do

I think often about the objects people handle and how they can pay off for us when we craft narratives. Today I'm thinking about a story by David Leavitt, "Gravity," about a young man, Theo, who has AIDS. He's opted for a sight-saving drug over the medications that will prolong his life. He's come home to live with his mother, and on the day of the story they've gone shopping for a wedding gift for Theo's cousin Howie. Theo's mother, Sylvia, insists on buying a $425 crystal bowl as a way of calling attention to the cheap pen and pencil set that Howie's mother gave Theo for his graduation. The extravagant bowl will serve as a reminder to Howie's mother that Sylvia hasn't forgotten the slight.

In the gift shop Sylvia picks up the bowl. "You have to feel it," she says to Theo. Then she tosses it to him, throws it "like a football." The store clerks hold their breath and look on in horror. Theo catches the bowl, letting his cane rattle to the floor; his arms sink with the weight of the crystal. Sylvia takes the bowl from him and carries it to the counter. She pays for it with "a look of relish" on her face. This section of the story ends with the line "It seemed Sylvia had been looking a long time for something like this, something heavy enough to leave an impression, yet so fragile it could make you sorry." Exactly. The bowl, a literal detail in the story, now shimmers with everything that's at stake. In narratives we can use a detail in a surprising way that allows it to hold the emotional or psychological interiors of the characters.

An expensive bowl in a story. What to do with it (for we must put our details to work)? Leavitt wisely chooses to have a character do the thing least expected—to throw that bowl to her feeble, dying son. I'm not sure we expect him to catch it, but he does. Leavitt himself holds onto that bowl through the closing part of the narrative. Sometimes we let go too soon of a detail we've put to use. We seduce ourselves into thinking that the strange thing is enough, that the memorable comes from the oddity. As Leavitt shows us at the end of "Gravity," our details can take us to resonant places inside our characters if we're willing to stay with them.

Back in the car the fraught nature of what might have happened when Sylvia tossed that bowl lingers. The incident in the store never leaves us, nor does it leave Theo and Sylvia. She asks him where else they might go. She insists there must be somewhere else. He reminds her it's almost time for his medicine and they should go home. This is the moment when her facade cracks. The thrill of the danger avoided in the tossing of the bowl can no longer hold: "For just a moment, but perceptibly, her face broke. She squeezed her eyes shut so tight the blue eye shadow on her lids cracked. . . . Almost as quickly she was back to normal again, and they were driving. 'It's getting hotter,' Sylvia said. 'Shall I put on the air?'"

We must have genuine emotion in our narratives but never sentimentality. A reader should never feel that he or she is being forced to feel something. It all has to rise organically from the story itself. Taking our cue from Leavitt, we can let dialogue, action, and details bring the emotion to the surface. Then we can cover it over by allowing our characters to reconstruct the masks that they wear. Sylvia is close to sobbing at the thought of all that's ahead, but she squeezes her eyes shut and gets back to normal. The sadness is now felt more deeply by the readers because we know it's there, silent, beneath the facade.

Leavitt also knows how to let the detail open up the interiority of his main character, Theo. In the last move of the story he's thinking about that bowl and all it represents: "There are certain things you've already done before you even think how to do them—a child pulled from in front of a car, for instance, or the bowl, which Theo was holding before he could even begin to calculate its brief trajectory. It had pulled his arms down, and from that apish posture he'd looked at his mother, who smiled broadly, as if, in the war between heaviness and shattering, he'd just helped her win some small but sustaining victory." When there are complicated emotions at work in our narratives, sometimes the best way to express them is to let our characters put a detail to work. A mother throws an expensive crystal bowl to her dying son; the sadness, the fierceness, is suddenly everywhere without the need of direct statement.

The Places We Know

What Richard Ford Taught Me

It took me a good while as a writer to trust the world I knew best—that world of small farms and towns and the men and women who worked hard at jobs that didn't pay them nearly enough. Sometimes those people lived too large for their own good. Sometimes they made poor choices and suffered the consequences. They cut each other with knives, they burned down buildings just for the thrill of it, they left families to run off with someone not their wife or husband, they ended up in prison, they took a deal from a judge and went to the army to avoid ending up in prison, they lived lonely lives of regret because once upon a time they'd had a chance to really be somebody and then, like the years, that chance just went away. Despite whatever wrong turns they took or lives they wished for, they often found joy in the most simple things: a few hands of pitch around a kitchen table, an ice cream social at the Methodist church, a tenderloin sandwich carried home in a paper bag from Bea's Café.

That was the world I knew most intimately—knew it inside my skin—that world of ordinary living pierced by sudden violence, that world of simple beauty set against the brutality people could visit upon it, but when I was a young writer trying to find my voice and my material, I erroneously thought that no one would ever be interested in the stories I knew best. Why would anyone want to read about those itty-bitty towns and farms and the people who lived there?

Then I met Richard Ford. I was living in Memphis at the time, and there was a book expo being held at the Peabody Hotel. I knew that one of my former teachers, Jim Whitehead, was going to be among the featured authors, so I decided to go down in hopes of saying hello. As luck would have it, I'd no more than stepped into the lobby when the elevator door opened and out stepped Jim. He was a burly man with a big heart and a booming voice, and when he saw me, he clapped me on the shoulder, told me how good it was to see me (it had been three years since I'd been in Jim's workshop at the University of Arkansas), and said, "Come in here." He motioned to the ballroom where the authors would sit behind tables and sign books for folks. He got me a chair and told me to sit down and keep him company. Then he spotted Richard Ford, and he introduced me to him. I remember that Ford was soft-spoken and gracious, and though I was nothing to him, he took the time to shake my hand and chat a little. He didn't make me feel that I was a nuisance or someone he had to make small talk with while he waited for the bigger fish to arrive. He treated me with respect, genuinely wanting to know a little bit about me. He had a quiet dignity that was disarming and a way of making me feel that my life, at that moment, was something that very much interested him. His story collection *Rock Springs* had just come out, and of course, I bought a copy, which he kindly inscribed: "With the pleasure it was to meet you and with the best wishes for your work." That book changed me as a writer forever.

Although the stories in that collection are for the most part set in the American West, they were about the sort of people I knew from my native Midwest. They were people in all sorts of dire straits, but they were doing their best to figure a way out, and the narrative voice I heard—a voice similar to the one I'd heard from Ford himself that day in Memphis: dignified, humble, curious, gracious—taught me how to tell the stories of ordinary people, to tell, more specifically, the stories of the people who mattered most to me. It took Ford, a southerner writing about the West, to take me home to southern Illinois in my writing. He taught me that the individual life mattered and would be of extreme interest to a reader if I treated it with respect, if I didn't turn away from its simultaneous ugliness and beauty, and if I wrote with forgiveness.

I've lost patience with writers who fall prey to the current gimmicks just for the sake of a little flash and flare and a chance to feel on the cutting edge of a trend. It seems to me that we should be in the game for larger stakes than the pyrotechnics of language or the clever shifting of form. Of course, those things sometimes align themselves nicely with what a particular writer must confront in the world around him or her and, therefore, become essential to their necessary exploration, but I've seen too many young writers fall back upon tricks of language and form to keep themselves from having to give shape to the mysteries of the complicated and compelling worlds they occupy. I know I sound like a curmudgeon now, having lived long enough, I suppose, to earn the right to wag a finger or two, but sometimes I think there are fewer and fewer of us holding the fort in the camp of realism these days, and for me that's where the real stakes are and will always be. The day-to-day living in the real world, even for those seemingly ordinary people on my farms and in my small midwestern towns, is rich and mysterious with desire, thwarted more often than not by poor choices and circumstances but still pulsing and well-worth examination.

Richard Ford, in those *Rock Springs* stories, taught me to look closely at what mattered most to me in the places I knew as home.

Daydreaming Your Memoir

I saw a photograph once, but now it only exists in my memory. It was an 8" x 10" glossy of the congregation of the Berryville Church of Christ, the church I attended with my mother when I was a small child living on our family farm. The church itself was a one-room affair with a brick chimney and whitewashed clapboards. It sat a little ways south of Berryville proper, which is to say it was just a bit south of the Berryville General Store. My grandparents at one time managed that store. They lived kitty-corner from it in a modest frame house. In March 1956 my grandfather came home from church on a Sunday evening, had a heart attack, and died. I was five months old, and I would know him only through the things he left behind, the things I found later when I spent my preschool days in my grandmother's care—the cigarette lighters and pipe cleaners; the glass paperweights and the Bicycle playing cards; the Zane Grey novels and the concrete wishing well he'd built in the yard.

I wish I could see that photograph again. I wish I'd known my grandfather. I wish I could call back all the people who stood in front of that small church on what must have been a cold day, given the coats and head scarves the women wore—the long coats with their fake fur collars, the scarves with their floral prints. Some of the women wore snow boots, the kind they slipped on over their regular shoes. The men wore overcoats and fedoras. I can smell the damp wool and the scents of tobacco and coal smoke. My grandmother wore a hairnet. Her black pocketbook dangled from her wrist. She crossed her hands over her ample stomach. The women smelled of talcum powder and Aqua Net hairspray. They wore rimless spectacles or cat's-eye glasses. I clung to the folds of my mother's coat. I had on a light-gray jacket that zipped up the front, a gray cap with ear flaps turned down and a strap fastened beneath my chin.

Forced to remember these details, I quickly begin to remember others. Delbar Tarpley sang hymns in a loud voice. He never sat with his wife, Ruth, who was my Sunday school teacher. The communion bread was a round of pie crust, from which everyone broke a small piece. After the service the children got whatever was left. The "wine" was Welch's Grape Juice served in a single glass goblet from which everyone sipped. When the offering was made, we all marched to the front of the church while singing a hymn and placed a few coins in a basket. An out-of-town relative might actually put in a bill or two. For the most part we were farming families who didn't have much to spare. I remember the names: Tarpley, Treece, McVeigh, Sanders, Read, Martin. Here we all are, forever caught in memory.

For the memoirist the past exists in what's often a haze, but it's our job to make something specific and vivid from the fog of our memories. Sometimes we have the benefit of documents or photographs to help us, but sometimes we don't. Sometimes we only have the memory of something seen or experienced. When that memory is vague or when we're not sure we can trust it, we should start with one detail—long coats with fake fur collars, a deck of Bicycle playing cards—and let that detail conjure others until we're daydreaming ourselves back into the world of memory or feeling ourselves become a part of times and places we never knew.

So often I hear my student writers say they don't have good memories and they can't recall the things they wish they could when they write memoir. Somehow I always doubt that. I wonder whether they're trying too hard to remember. Relax, I want to tell them. All you have to do is daydream. Go back in time, remember one object, one scent, one taste, one sound. Every scene begins with one something that begets another something and another and another until finally the fabric of the memory has become whole and achingly real on the page. Memoirists reconstruct their lives one detail at a time. The people in the photograph I'll probably never again see? They're not going anywhere. They're frozen in time. With all patience they wait for me to remember them.

The Heart's Field

Place in Fiction

I grew up in a place where people came to town on Saturday nights to do their trading. My father loafed with the other men in Tubby's barbershop or Buzz Eddie's pool hall and then went out to sit on the bench on the corner, still shooting the shit, while my mother and I pushed a cart up and down the aisle of Ferguson's market or Spec Atkins's Grocery, laying in what we needed for the week ahead. The gully on our farm where we tossed what we couldn't burn of our trash was full of Wagner's juice jars, blue Milk of Magnesia bottles (my father had a nervous stomach), Log Cabin syrup bottles, Indian Summer Cider jugs.

We did our trading because we worked like mules all week. We worked hard and got put up wet. We took our baths in galvanized washtubs on Saturday nights. We stayed up late and watched Championship Wrestling on WTVW out of Evansville, Indiana, our TV rotor set at SE. We listened to high school basketball games on the radio in the winter. We sat at our kitchen tables, which were covered with vinyl oilcloths, and ate apple slices and corn popped over a gas burner on the stove. We yelled at the radio when a call didn't go our team's way. "Give him a saddle, ref. He's riding him." "Ah, you're blind out of one eye and can't see good out of the other."

My mother scrubbed her head, did rubbings of laundry. My father said, "If ifs and buts were candies and nuts, we'd all have a merry Christmas." He said, "People in hell wanting ice water too," whenever I whined about something I didn't have and wanted. "Mister, you're breeding a scab on your nose," he'd say if I whined too much. Sometimes we were a day late and a dollar short. Other times we were told to shit or get off the pot, straighten up and fly right, or else someone would jerk knots in our tails.

We were a farm family in southeastern Illinois. We had our sayings, and we had our ways.

Fish frys; pancake suppers; chowders; ice cream socials; bridal showers with mixed nuts and butter mints; Tupperware parties; donkey basketball games; auctions; meetings of the Odd Fellows, the Moose, the Elks, the Masons, the Rebekah Lodge; bingo games at the American Legion; demolition derbies and harness races and tractor pulls at the county fair.

To quote Flannery O'Connor: "There are two qualities that make fiction. One is the sense of mystery and the other is the sense of manners. You get the manners from the texture of existence that surrounds you."

Stories that seem like they could happen anywhere actually seem to not be happening at all. What is the texture of existence in the places that you know best? What are the customs, the language, the social expectations, the geographical landscape, the demands and pleasures of climate, the idiosyncrasies? Characters usually act in accordance with, or resistance to, the places where they live, and once they do, they set a narrative in motion.

So, that story (or novel, essay, poem, play, screenplay) you're working on? Make sure you've gathered the details of the setting, not just the sensory details but the facts of language and custom as well. Put your main character in what O'Connor called "a believable and significant social context" and let one action lead to the next in this very specific place where people talk certain ways, do certain things, or else violate it all by stepping outside the expected.

"The truth is, fiction depends for its life on place," Eudora Welty wrote. "Location is the crossroads of circumstance, the proving ground of 'What happened? Who's here? Who's coming?'— and that is the heart's field." The uniqueness of place is endangered today. Builders construct houses according to a handful of models. Franchise restaurants and shops replace independently owned businesses. Don't even get me started on how the discount store Walmart has dried up the downtown business districts of thousands of small American towns. The truth is the landscape is becoming more and more homogeneous and predictable these days. Thank god for the artists, then, who remind us of the particulars of our world. Today, more than ever, it's important that writers understand how to evoke the unique qualities of landscapes by finding the details that distinguish them and then using those details to create characters, plots, atmospheres, and meaning. If you know your place fully, you'll understand how it becomes necessary to the characters, their stories, their emotions, and to everything you've come to the page to express.

Oh, Those Pesky Facts

What's a Memoir Writer to Do?

Let's admit it: anyone who writes memoir does a song and dance with the facts. Even if we're determined to be completely faithful and only include the verifiable when it comes to event, chronology, and dialogue, our memories are fallible, and sometimes they're the only thing we can rely on to say, "This is the truth."

To me this conversation about what to do with the facts starts to become tiresome but also necessary. When it comes to writing memoir, what are we willing to do with the facts of our lives? In addition, what should we not allow ourselves to do?

If you happen to believe that everything should be verifiable in a memoir, then here's a list of transgressions I've committed. I confess that I've created dialogue for characters, giving them things to say that I can't be sure they said at that exact time. I've also conveniently provided them with props and details; I've never given anyone something they never had, but perhaps I have them use a prop or wear a certain hat or make a certain gesture at a time that I feel will help dramatize the moment I'm putting on the page. Truth be told, I've also tinkered with chronology for the benefit of the narrative arc. I've collapsed or telescoped time; I've rearranged sequence. I'm a storyteller; this is what I do.

Consider this scene in my book-length memoir *From Our House.* I'm eleven years old, and during the weeks that summer I'm living alone with my father on our farm while my mother is an hour away in Charleston at Eastern Illinois University, finishing her bachelor's degree. In the scene I'm helping my father work on a piece of machinery. On this day my wrench slips, and I scrape my hand. My father says, "You want me to make you a sugar tit?"

I have to admit that I'm not sure that he really said that at that exact moment, but it's true that he said it to me often when I was growing up, wanting to call attention to the fact that I needed to toughen up. While writing this scene, the pressure between us got built up, and for the sake of the narrative momentum, I wanted him to say something that would precipitate the action. Because this was something he often said, I decided to use that line of dialogue to drive the engine of this scene in which I try to walk away from him (true), he takes off his belt to whip me (true), I catch the belt in my hand and tug it away from him. This last action didn't happen during the sequence of events that I'm dramatizing. It happened during another moment sometime in the future. It lodged in my memory, the feeling of taking that belt from my father, and I decided to use it out of sequence to better motivate the ensuing action.

In the written scene my father looks at me, first with surprise and then with a growing anger. He steps toward me, and I run down our lane. He chases after me, but he can't keep up, and soon I find myself alone at the end of the lane, knowing eventually I'll have to go back. It's that moment of wanting to escape and knowing I never really can that holds the complicated feelings of a boy who simultaneously loved and feared his father. That was the story of this time of our lives; this scene is meant to take me deep into that feeling, and I found that inventing that line of dialogue and rearranging the chronology to provide clearer emotional triggers for the action became necessary for taking me to the complicated truth of what it was to be my father's son.

But before you think me unethical, let me say that there were other times in the writing of this memoir when I found myself giving my father lines of dialogue that were unfair to him, lines that came from my negative feelings toward him, lines that portrayed him in a singular dimension of anger and cruelty that took me over the ethical line of nonfiction and into the realm of fiction. Those were the moments when I had to step back and rewrite to make sure I was portraying my father accurately. We all know where these ethical lines are when we write memoir, and we know that funny feeling inside us when we cross them. We have to pay attention to those feelings; we have to make sure we haven't played loose with the facts for our own purposes rather than for the sake of the truthful things we can express about the mysteries and complexities of our experiences.

And what of those facts that are ordinary and on the surface uninteresting? How can we put them to use in our memoirs? In the next section following the scene I've just described, I write about how I took care of my father that summer and how on Fridays we stopped work early and got cleaned up so we could drive to Charleston to pick up my mother. I write about how I brought a basin of water to my father's bedroom and washed his naked body. When I was finished, "I rolled fresh white cotton arm socks over his stumps and safety-pinned them to his T-shirt sleeves. I helped him slip his arms into the holsters of his hooks and then settle the canvas straps of the harness across his back." These ordinary details—ordinary for us, anyway—stand alone in this quiet place after the drama of the preceding scene. The description of me washing and dressing my father shows the complicated truth of love's persistence in the face of cruelty. I have no need to rearrange or invent. The facts do the work. They take me to this truth: "How could I not love him, then, so great was his need."

So, the truth? Sometimes the facts can serve us well, but sometimes a few minor adjustments can serve the story better and more forcefully lead us to what we've come to the page to explore, to interrogate, to dramatize, as we finally know in our heart of hearts a deeper layer of truth rising up through the surfaces of our lives.

Memoir and the Work of Resurrection

I have a piece of wood, nearly six feet in length, taken from the debris of a farmhouse fallen in on itself. The farmhouse that belonged to my family, the house in which my mother first read to me, the house where I listened to my father and my uncles swap stories, the house where I would eventually spend long summer days reading books inherited from my grandfather, the house where my family suffered the accident that cost my father both of his hands, the house that he filled with his rage.

This piece of wood is ragged along the bottom edge. A piece of wood nearly a hundred years old, but now, thanks to the imagination and the sure hand of someone who cares, this piece of wood displays my family's name, along with the description of the location in the exact language of the original deed that showed my great-grandfather's ownership of this land: South ½ of the Northwest ¼ of Section 18, Township 2 North, Range 13 West of the Second Prime Meridian. At the far edge of the wood is a replica of the plat map of Lukin Township, Lawrence County, Illinois, complete with skeins of blue paint to represent the waterways, one of which is the creek that cut across our eighty acres and where I first learned to identify the tracks of raccoons, coyotes, deer.

It takes a good deal of love to preserve something. The memoirist knows this work, the work of resurrection. To put our lives on the page, even the most bitter parts of them, takes a tremendous amount of faith and love—faith that the work matters, love for the people we were and are and will be. It takes attention and fidelity to rescue the distant parts of our lives.

We who write memoirs should remind ourselves that we tell our stories not from bitterness or anger but from the desire to record, to document, to explore, to make sense of, to portray what's universal in our individual experiences, to say, *Once there was a life*. We must go about our work with the respect that our lives deserve. This means looking closely, this means finding the stories that we need to know more about, this means taking our time to dramatize those moments fully, this means loving all the parts of our experiences enough to make them live again.

I have a picture of my father as a little boy, probably around 1920, outside the farmhouse. The piece of wood is one of those clapboards. My father is slack-jawed, staring at the camera, in a sort of wonder perhaps that someone has come to take his photograph. What magic it must be to this boy, this country boy, to know that the camera will put his image on a paper that anyone will be able to see. Here is this boy, here is this house, here are all the years between then and now. Here is this piece of wood, rescued and preserved, to hang now where I live.

Using Photos in Memoir

I remember on New Year's Eve, when I was a boy, my father's side of the family would gather for a supper of oyster soup and games of cards—usually either pitch or rook. This was in a day when we didn't have cell phones that took pictures, when we didn't live in a society that immediately documents every moment. On occasion someone would have an instamatic camera or a Polaroid, so sometimes there would be a few moments frozen in time—people sitting around a kitchen table, cards fanned before them, my cousin reaching out to gather in a trick or my mother in the midst of conversation, her head tossed back as she laughed.

These days we take countless photos and post them to social media or just leave them on our cameras or erase them, and it seems to me that we've made our experiences fleeting and disposable. In the days when photos were fewer, they meant more, particularly for the memoirist, who years later studies these pictures for the stories they tell or the ones that they don't.

When beginning to write a memoir, it's often a good idea to gather photographs from the time in question. Looking at these pictures not only immerses you in the time period; it also provides an emotional connection between you and the people about whom you're writing.

Here are some things that can happen while looking at old photos:

1. A photograph can suggest a scene. You look at the clothes people wore, the way someone held his or her hands, the things on the wall of the kitchen, the radio on top of the refrigerator, the old percolator in the corner and suddenly from these details people begin to move and talk.

2. A photograph can suggest other scenes. You look at the picture and remember the night of the New Year's Eve party, and that memory triggers other memories, and the next thing you know you're constructing a narrative.

3. A photograph can make you curious. Why did your father's eyeglasses never fit properly? Why didn't he take the time to get them adjusted? What does that one detail say about the story of your family?

4. A photograph can suggest the secrets your family tried to keep. What does that pained smile on your mother's face try to cover over? What do you know about her that's there just below the surface of the photograph?

5. A photograph can carry you forward into the present. What would that New Year's Eve party be like now if everyone would have been allowed to live and you could interact with them as the adult you are? How does that moment from years ago connect to the person you are now?

For the memoirist old photos can be keys to making your writing a vivid inquiry into past, present, and future. Meaning resides in those photos. If we start with them, we'll be well on our way to finding what they contain. Photos can document experience while also sparking our imagination. Take the time to look, to remember, to question, to think, and to imagine.

Ordinary Details in Memoir

My mother, when she was in her last years, had a habit of sitting in her chair, her hands on the arms, her fingers lifting and pressing down, one by one, as if she were playing scales on the piano. She'd never played a piano. In fact, she had no musical talent at all.

She was a soft-spoken sort, long on patience and kindness and compassion. She believed in the Golden Rule. She was a Christian woman who endured my father's temper and my battles with him until finally both he and I saw how wrong we were and became the sort of men she deserved to have in her house.

But I was telling you about her fingers and the way they went back and forth, up and down, as she sat quietly in her chair. Upon first glance, at least the way I've presented this detail so far, it's an ordinary moment that I'm describing: my mother sitting in her chair, looking at the television, the lamplight falling over her. How many times had I seen her like that, enjoying a moment of rest? She was a third grade teacher for thirty-eight years, and after her retirement she worked in the laundry and the kitchen of a nursing home. Somehow she managed to help my father on our farm and to keep house and to raise a son. Why should I remember this particular moment?

Those fingers and the way they moved. Such a small detail, ordinary, barely worth noticing, unless you're her son and all this happens on one of the last days your mother will know you.

Her dementia had worsened after a series of small strokes, and she wasn't able to live by herself any longer. I was her only child, and I'd had to make the decision nobody wants to make, that she should live in a nursing home. I'd seen her move her fingers like that before and never thought a thing about it. It was just a habit she had, the same way she knelt by her bed each night and prayed before going to bed or the odd way she had of accenting the syllables of certain words: ca-SHEW, il-LUS-trated, to-FU. Or the unique way she answered the phone with a rousing "Yello."

Those fingers, up and down and back and forth. Suddenly, though I'd seen her move her fingers that way countless times, I understood that she knew this was one of the last nights she'd spend in her home. Something was at war within her, something most likely that had to do with her belief in civility and the fear she felt. She worked those fingers to keep from saying something she'd regret.

On the night I'm recalling, the mail carrier had mistakenly delivered a parcel meant for someone down the street. My mother insisted on taking the parcel to her neighbor. By this time it was dark. I told her not to worry about the parcel; I'd make sure it got to the rightful recipient the next day.

That's when she clapped her hands together. The noise startled me. "All right, then," she said. "If it doesn't get to where it's supposed to go, I won't be the one to blame."

I remember how her voice shook with anger, how tears came to her eyes. There we were at one of the extraordinary moments that will be with me as long as I live. I can't forget it. I can't ever forget how my mother insisted on doing the right thing at a time when she must have felt so wronged and wounded. I can't forget the jumble of emotions that rose up in me when she clapped her hands and said what she did.

Memoirs are made from moments like this, those moments that shake us, perplex us, change us, or give us opportunities that we don't take and so they go shooting past us forever, never to come again. But memoirs are also made from the commonplace, from ordinary details that provide a backdrop from which the unforgettable moments emerge. My mother's fingers, the clapping of her hands, the accusation that she made: all of that exists alongside the crossword puzzles she liked to do, the shopping lists she made on the backs of calendar pages, the Halls cough drops she kept in her purse, the deliberate way she shuffled a deck of cards, the Dear Abby advice columns she liked to read. Every ordinary detail of the lived life is necessary to the extraordinary moments that we remember, that haunt us perhaps, the ones that demand our attention when we set out to tell the tale. We have to pay attention to the commonplace so we'll better recognize the variations within it. Sometimes a simple action signifies everything if we're watching closely enough.

Connecting Particulars

The poet and essayist Sydney Lea offered some thoughts on what he called the "lyrical essay" in an article that appeared in the *Writer's Chronicle* in February 1999. This was early on in the explosion of the lyric essay that has continued with the work of such writers as Eula Biss, Jenny Boully, John D'Agata, Ander Monson, and many others, but Lea's thoughts on how an essayist works by the art of indirection, dealing with seemingly disparate particulars as he or she writes toward a point of connection, are still extremely relevant to this form as it's practiced today.

Lea talked about the importance of having no predetermined subject, only a handful of particular details that have lodged in the essayist's consciousness. He pointed out how the lyric essayist does better when he or she doesn't know where the essay is headed so that observations have the feel of spontaneity. The meditative impulse of the essay places an emphasis on the writer's mind in action with perception unfolding in the act of writing, an act of what Lea called "unanticipated discovery." He stressed the importance of beginning with particulars before leaping into meditation, contemplation, musing, reminiscing, preaching, worrying, arguing, and perhaps even pontificating. We begin, in other words, with what the poet Miller Williams calls the "furniture of the world." "I find that certain things have lodged themselves in my consciousness," Lea wrote, "and now demand meditation, that they have 'subjected' *me*." The lyric essayist seeks to connect a number of images or moments that won't leave him or her alone. In the process of writing, Lea pointed out, referencing Robert Frost, "we discover what we didn't know we knew."

With the lyric impulse in mind, I offer this brief writing activity.

Our objective here is to get down the bare bones of a short lyric essay, knowing that we'll go back later and fill in the connective tissue, the meditation, and other elements.

1. Choose a particular detail that has lodged in your mind, anything from the world around you: a dandelion, a crack in your bedroom wall, the man who lives in the house on the corner. Write one statement about this object or person. Perhaps it begins with the words "I see it [or him or her] for the first time . . . ."

2. Quick! Before you have time to think, list two other particulars suggested by the one you recalled in step 1. Write them in the margin or at the top of the page.

3. Write a statement about one of the particulars from your list. Perhaps your sentence begins, "One day I notice . . . ."

4. Write one sentence, more abstract, in response to either or both of the particulars that have made their way into your essay draft. Let the gaze turn inward. Perhaps you begin with the words "I've always wondered about . . . ."

5. Write a statement about a third particular. Put yourself into action. Perhaps you begin with something like "Tonight, I walk . . . ."

6. Close with a statement of abstraction, a bold statement perhaps. We'll hope this will be the moment in which you discover how these three particulars connect. Maybe it's a line like the one that ends Linda Hogan's short essay "Walking": "You are the result of the love of thousands."

The lyric impulse requires the writer to trust in leaps and associations as he or she works with what may seem to be disparate images, details, and memories. In the act of considering, the writer invites the reader to follow the sensibility that will eventually find a moment that resonates with the significance that these particulars generate when held next to one another. That juxtaposition actually makes possible a conversation between the particulars, a conversation that's taking the writer and the reader to a place neither could have predicted when the essay began.

Please feel free to take the sentences from this exercise and expand your essay in whatever way pleases you.

Context

One day, when the writing just wouldn't come, I gave up and went out to mow the yard. I noticed a Tonka Truck dump truck in the yard across the street, and later I saw the shell of a cicada clinging to the purple bloom of a blazing star, and through those two details I started to go somewhere I hadn't known I would.

When I was a boy, I had a Tonka Truck like the one in the yard across the street. The bed of the truck in my neighbor's yard was raised, as if the load had been delivered and soon the driver would lower it and move on down the road. I also collected the shells of cicadas when I was a boy, finding them clinging to the limbs of trees.

I imagine there are a number of folks who share those experiences: the joy of a Tonka Truck, the fascination with those cicada shells. To say I had a Tonka Truck when I was a boy or that I collected cicada shells has little resonance for a listener, outside the shared nostalgia for our childhoods now gone. Neither statement tells you anything about who I was as a boy or what my fears or dreams or secrets were. Those two sentences are as declarative as declarative can be. "I had a Tonka Truck when I was a boy." "I collected cicada shells." Nothing vibrates above or beneath them. They are merely facts.

The Tonka Truck in the yard across the street intrigues me because no children live in that house, nor do any children come to visit the man who lives there. The man is a troubled man. I'd say he's somewhere in his fifties. During the day he sits on his front steps, and I hear him talking to himself or else to whatever voices he hears inside his head. Sometimes he rants and rails against whatever it is that disturbs him.

Now he's taken to lying in the middle of the street late at

night. Recently I took the garbage can to the curb and found him on his back. I said, "Aren't you afraid a car might hit you?" He said, "They usually have their headlights on." He liked to lie there and look up at the stars, he said. "I wouldn't want to see you get hurt," I told him. He said, "I wouldn't want to see you get hurt either." Not sure whether he meant that as a threat or an expression of neighborly affection, I bid him good night and went back inside my house.

The cicada shell is amazing for its detail: the clear globes where the eyes once rested, the delicate threads of the antennae, the slit in the back through which the new cicada emerged, its clear wings laced with lime green skeins. The wings and the new body would harden in time, and the cicada would fly away, leaving the shell for me to find.

I remember the first time I spoke to the man across the street. I'd been mowing, and he'd yelled at me. I ignored him. Later he came to my door to apologize. He kept saying, "This is my neighborhood, and these are my neighbors," as if he were trying to remind himself of what kept him anchored to this world.

Details are nothing without context. What we carry inside us matters, and details resonate when they allow the importance of all that we can't say to emerge. I think of my neighbor lying in the street, looking at the stars. I think of that Tonka Truck, the bed lifted, in his yard. I consider a grown man perhaps dreaming of his own childhood, perhaps eager to unburden himself of whatever haunts him now. I think of how desperately we sometimes long to escape. I pick up the cicada shell and place it on my palm. It rests there, balanced on its legs, such a light and brittle thing.

PART 4 ❧ Point of View

"Little Pig, Little Pig, Let Me Come In"

I have wanted you to see out of
my eyes so many times.

—ELIZABETH BERG

Your Point of View Choice Creates
the Effect of the Story

I was talking with a student once who'd decided to tell a story from a collective consciousness, the voice of the "we." Perhaps the most well-known example of this strategy in short fiction is the Faulkner story, "A Rose for Emily," which begins by establishing the perspective of the Mississippi town in which Emily Grierson has lived and died: "When Miss Emily Grierson died, our whole town went to her funeral; the men through a sort of respectful affection for a fallen monument, the women mostly out of curiosity to see the inside of her house, which no one, save an old manservant—a combined gardener and cook—had seen in at least ten years."

Notice how this opening not only sets up the collective point of view of the town but also divides that perspective into two subsets: the perspective of the men in town and the perspective of the women. The point of view can then shift slightly within that collective consciousness depending on what is called for at a certain point. A contingent of men can visit Miss Emily's house when she doesn't pay her taxes, and within that scene we can see Miss Emily in action through the point of view of "the men": "They rose when she entered—a small, fat woman in black, with a thin gold chain descending to her waist and vanishing into her belt, leaning on her ebony cane with a tarnished gold head." And we can hear her speak for herself, engaging in dialogue with the men:

> She did not ask them to sit. She just stood in the door and listened quietly until the spokesman came to a stumbling halt. Then they could hear the invisible watch ticking at the end of the gold chain.

Her voice was dry and cold. "I have no taxes in Jefferson. Colonel Sartoris explained it to me. Perhaps one of you can gain access to the city records and satisfy yourselves."

"But we have. We are the city authorities, Miss Emily. Didn't you get a notice from the sheriff, signed by him?"

The scene goes on much the way any scene of dialogue and action would in a story, but in this case everything is filtered through the perspective of the men. Miss Emily turns them away, insisting that she has no taxes. A few of the women in town try to pay her a visit, but she won't receive them, bringing out this response in a collective dialogue: "'Just as if a man—any man— could keep a kitchen properly,' the ladies said; so they were not surprised when the smell developed. It was another link between the gross, teeming world and the high and mighty Griersons."

The story unfolds in this manner, the point of view never dipping into a single character's consciousness. There's a mystery about what's happened to Homer Barron, the construction foreman who's taken to squiring Miss Emily around. That mystery is finally solved at the end of the story, when, after Miss Emily's death, the townspeople force open the door to a room "in that region above the stairs" and find the skeleton of Homer Barron on the bed and an indentation in the pillow beside his remains where "a long strand of iron-gray hair" indicates that Miss Emily used to lie there beside the skeleton. Furthermore, the townspeople, remembering the arsenic she bought from the druggist, claiming she needed it for rats, now understand that she used it to kill Homer Barron. He wasn't the marrying kind, the story tells us, but it began to look, from the evidence gathered by the townspeople, that he and Miss Emily were making wedding preparations. The last time anyone spotted Homer Barron was when a neighbor saw Miss Emily's servant "admit him at the kitchen door one evening." The townspeople assume that the "quality of her father which had thwarted her woman's life so many times had been too virulent and too furious to die." It's clear that Miss Emily had this one last chance at love and familial expectations kept her from enjoying a married life with Homer Barron. What a poignant image that indentation in the pillow by Homer's skeleton is. What work the detail of that long strand of iron-gray hair does. Faulkner said in an interview once that the story came from a picture he had in his head of a strand of gray hair on a pillow. "It was a ghost story," he said. "Simply a picture of a strand of hair on the pillow in the abandoned house." It's a story of loneliness, of a desperate act, a tragic choice, a lifetime of consequences. All is revealed to the townspeople in that final image. All of it made a particular type of story because of the point of view choice.

The point of all of this? The lens through which we see a story creates a particular type of experience for us that couldn't be replicated with a different point of view choice. Faulkner's choice allows Miss Emily's despair and loneliness to wash over the townspeople. It casts her and her life in a very different light than was possible in the world of gossip and assumption. The very individual and private life made public carries with it a resonance that's hard to forget.

When we make a choice in point of view, we begin to create the overall effect of the story. Often this is an instinctual choice. We want, for example, to tell the story of something that had a significant effect on a central character, so we filter everything through his or her consciousness. Sometimes, though, we want to establish a completely different effect with the material at our disposal. We may want to broaden the lens of perception, as Faulkner did in "A Rose for Emily," to show how an event radiates through segments of a particular population or community, or we may want to work with an ironic effect only possible with the omniscient point of view. When we move away from the traditional first-person or third-person limited point of view to something less common, we should ask ourselves how that point of view choice allows us to best explore what interests us in a story and also how that choice makes possible the final effect of the narrative.

The Inner Story of the Writer's Thinking

I'm interested in the personae we create on the page of a piece of creative nonfiction as well as the way we go about building characters of depth, including our own character when we speak in a piece of memoir or a personal essay. I'm also interested in how successfully we wed form and content so that the shape of an essay best allows the expression of the writer's journey through its particulars.

Vivian Gornick, in her wonderful book about the craft of the memoir, *The Situation and the Story*, tells us that each piece of memoir has a situation, which she defines as "the context or circumstances, sometimes the plot." We might call this the surface subject or the apparent subject. Perhaps it's the narrative of the first time your mother took you bowling, as is the case in Ira Sukrungruang's brief essay "Chop Suey." "The story," Gornick says, "is the emotional experience that preoccupies the writer: the insight, the wisdom, the thing one has come to say." Here we have what we might call the deeper subject, the one that rises through the pressures of the situation and particularly through the opposing aspects of the writer's sensibility. Ira's essay opens with statements of what he knew about his mother as they entered the El-Mar Bowling Alley one day. He knew she expected him "to be the perfect Thai boy." He knew that she didn't like the blonde American women she feared would seduce him. He knew "her distrust of the world she found herself in." Notice how the story, or the deeper subject, already exists in this opening. The statement about the mother's distrust of the American world sets the stage for what the drama of the narrative will produce, the deeper subject (or the "story," to use Gornick's terminology), which is one of ethnic considerations, dignity, pride, and parental protection. All of this works its way to the top through the tensions of the narrative.

Judith Kitchen says that in an essay we participate by paying attention to the consideration that the writer gives the material. In other words, we're interested in what Michael Steinberg calls "the inner story," or the story of the writer's thinking. We're interested in following the conversation that the writer is having between the various parts of the self as he or she reflects, inter-rogates, speculates, meditates, examines, digresses, projects, and acts as the interpreter of his or her own experience. The essayist, then, constructs a multilayered persona through which to best consider the thing he or she has come to the page to explore. Gornick calls this persona "the involuntary truth speaker, who implicates himself not because he wants to but because he has no choice." At some point the essayist needs to know who he or she is in any particular essay. Such knowledge, Gornick says, allows the writer to create a persona that best serves the insight that an essay finally expresses. In the case of "Chop Suey" it's the insight of the young Thai boy observing his mother's response to a racist man who means to belittle her but ends up being belittled him-self due to the mother's sharp use of irony. To achieve that turn at the end, Ira wisely creates the persona of the naive boy, who by the essay's end coexists with the wiser boy, someone more aware of racism and the dignified response to it that preserves dignity.

So, a quick writing activity to help generate some material while also providing the opportunity to put into practice some of the techniques relevant to characterization, persona, and the role of the truth speaker:

1. Recall a childhood memory from your early school days, something that you can't get out of your mind even though years have passed, something that's still somewhat unresolved, something that you regret, something that changed you, something that helped shape the person you are today. An object may help you recall such a moment:

a jar of paste, the braids of a girl in your class, a pair of scissors. Write some opening lines that use the object to set a narrative or a meditation into motion while at the same time beginning to create a persona on the page. An example from "Chop Suey": "My mother was a champion bowler in Thailand. This was not what I knew of her."

2. Write a few lines that further establish who you were at that period of your life. Begin, if you wish, with the words "I was . . . ." Fill in the blank in a way that gives you and the readers an idea of who you were within the moment that you're recalling. Reread the opening of "Chop Suey" for a clear example of this.

3. Articulate some mixed feelings relevant to what you're writing about by completing this prompt: "Part of me . . . but another part of me . . . ."

4. Write another few lines that return to the narrative or to the description of and meditation on the object with which you started. Feel the modulation of voice and persona as you move from what I'll call the dramatic present to the more reflective voice and then back.

5. Consider why you're writing about this moment in your life by completing the following prompt: "Maybe I can't forget . . . or maybe . . . ."

It's important, when writing a piece of memoir or a personal essay to establish early on who's speaking and for what purpose. To refer to Kitchen and Gornick again, your reader wants to be part of the attention being paid to a situation and to the story, or the deeper subject existing beneath it. We're interested not only in what happened but more so in what the writer makes of what happened. This requires a graceful movement between the person the writer was in the midst of the experience and the person the writer is now as he or she reflects on it. I hope this writing activity will help you feel that movement while also generating a piece of writing that you can continue to develop in your writing room.

136

Finding a Different Lens

To be honest, sometimes I worry about my returning to the story of my family over and over. I worry that readers will eventually tire of my writing about the accident that cost my father both of his hands when I was barely a year old and the rage he brought into our home throughout my childhood and on into my teenage years. Then I think about what a notable writer said—maybe it was Fitzgerald, maybe it was Flaubert (some of you will surely know)—about a writer being lucky to figure out early on what his obsessions were and to spend a lifetime writing about them.

No single event in my life has shaped the rest of it the way my father's accident did. I keep trying to write myself out of it, but I never quite succeed. That's why I have to go back and tell it again. The key to writing about the same material over and over is to find a fresh perspective. I try to change the camera's lens. For example, I just finished an essay about my grandmother—my father's mother—and her blindness and her belief in the faith healer Oral Roberts. Through her story I approach the story of my father in this piece called "The Healing Line." The central event of the narrative is a moment I've written before from my own perspective. Writing about it this time, I look at it through my grandmother's perspective, through the circumstances of her life, and I find something new because I do that.

In another newly finished essay, my father's story comes to the page through the story of a night when a strange young man, lost and confused, came into our house. I use his desperation, his cry for help, his reaching out to my mother, as a way of thinking about the secret anger we were trying to keep hidden inside our home.

My key, then, to revisiting the same material numerous times is to always find a different lens through which to see that which won't leave me alone. My obsession, it seems, is never ending, as, of course, true obsessions always are, but the position from which I see is always moving, using different characters or situations as my viewfinder. The end result for me is a fuller picture of my own experience. I learn something new with each essay that I write. If the material is richly complicated, as this story of my family is, I'm not sure one will ever run out of new ways to explore it as long as the writer is open to the slightly off-center perspective that other characters or stylistic choices can provide.

Memoir and the Future

A few days ago I was telling my cousin that I used to have problems managing my anger. She asked me what I'd done to let that anger go. Without thinking, I said I wrote a book called *From Our House*. It's true. Writing that memoir about my father's farming accident, the angry man he became, the violence he brought into our home, our difficult relationship, and our eventual journey toward reconciliation allowed me to gain a measure of control over the temper that living with my father's rage instilled in me.

I wrote *From Our House* on a laptop while sitting in my La-Z-Boy recliner in my study. Day by day I dramatized the story of my family, often re-creating moments that made me uncomfortable to recall. I didn't hold back. I did the necessary work, and as I did, I simultaneously lived inside the drama the way I had as a child and also stood to the side and looked at that drama with a more interpretative eye, one that explored the question of how my family came to be the family that it was.

I told myself to be honest and fair. I challenged myself to see the good parts of my father and my relationship with him while at the same time dramatizing all that had been ugly and painful. When I finished the first draft, with the moment of when I knew my mother's faith and endurance and love would finally pay off for my family, I wept. I felt something lift from me, and I knew it was the anger that I thought I'd put aside all those years ago, when my father and I somehow silently agreed to live a more congenial life. I didn't know then that it would stay with me for years and years thereafter or that it would take a journey back to the past through the art of memoir to finally release it. I'll say it plain: writing *From Our House* saved me.

Which leads me to some thoughts about how that happened:

1. Dramatizing our experiences makes it impossible for us to avoid them. When we put them on the page, we fully own them. We make "public" (even if we never publish what we've written) what we've previously kept secret.

2. Once we've dramatized these previously secret moments, we have to make sure not to look away. As we leave one scene, we'd be smart to spend some time reflecting on the experience we've just rendered, interrogating it if necessary to see what we couldn't see at the time we were living it. Writing a memoir requires us to think, question, and interpret in ways we usually don't when we're inside the moments of our lives.

3. The more reflective voice of memoir invites us to practice the art of empathy. When I opened *From Our House* with imagining the moment of my father's accident from his perspective, I saw the source of his anger. I lived inside his skin. At that point it became possible for me to understand in some measure what it was like for him to live his life. Understanding doesn't have to lead to forgiveness, but it can . . .

4. . . . and if it doesn't, it can at least allow us to stop obsessing, stop reliving those hurtful moments from our pasts. We can let them go. We can see that we have power over the way we choose to allow our past experiences to affect our present lives. We can contain the past on the pages of a memoir. We can close the book. We can become different people. We can move forward, without resentment or embarrassment, into the future.

Living Full

Avoiding Sentimentality in Memoir

I received a triumphant message from a friend this morning about a breakthrough with the memoir she's writing. She reports "a strange and wonderful happening," the shedding of tears as she wrote, tears that came from the clear memory of her at a previous time, a time retrieved through the careful cataloging of specific concrete details. "I'm elated," my friend said, and anyone who's had a similar experience while writing a memoir will understand exactly what she's feeling, that emotional immersion into the past, an experience my friend described as "living full."

Yes, exactly. We live full when we slip into our past lives. The tears that come tell us we've arrived with our whole bodies. Although it might be sad to revisit the people we were in times of trouble, it's also a cause for celebration. So much conspires to keep us from slipping through the veil between the here and the then. When we finally break through, it indeed gives us, as my friend reported, a feeling of elation.

I remember well the moments during the writing of my first memoir, *From Our House*, in which the past seemed so real to me that I broke down in tears (yes, it's all right for male memoirists to cry). One such moment came when I was writing about the summer I lived alone with my father while my mother spent the weekdays at Eastern Illinois University, where she was finishing her degree. Those weeks my father and I spent alone on our farm were strange ones for us both; never before had we had so much time together without my mother to act as a buffer. "That summer I did for him what she would do for twenty-six years without regret or complaint," I write. "I shaved him, I bathed him, I cleaned him after he used the toilet." It wasn't recalling the intimacy of these actions that brought tears to my eyes; it was, instead, my father's vulnerability as I washed him. I remember how this memory overwhelmed me and how I had to find an appropriate measure of distance to be able to portray it without becoming maudlin. Which brings me to my point. We writers of memoir need the sort of immersion that sometimes brings us to tears, but we also need strategies for tempering the rawness of emotion so it becomes more deeply felt by the reader. In the passage about washing my father, I relied on a shift to a third-person point of view: "They would have seen the boy . . . ." That slight adjustment in perspective allowed me to be both the participant (the boy I was in the past) and the spectator (the adult who observes from a slight remove). As the spectator, I note the washcloth, the basin of water, the sunlight through the window, the boy's small hands, the father's nakedness. As the participant, I feel again the bashfulness, the love, the need. The blend of immersion and distance creates a moment on the page that not only I but also the reader can "live full."

Of course, this use of the third-person is only one strategy for blending perspectives in memoir. I've always found the voice of a calm narrator, blending with the voice of an intense moment, to be key. Anton Chekhov, in a letter to Lydia Avilova, offered this advice: "When you describe the miserable and unfortunate, and want to make the reader feel pity, try to be somewhat colder—that seems to give a kind of background to another's grief, against which it stands out more clearly. Whereas in your story the characters cry and you sigh. Yes, be more cold. . . . The more objective you are, the stronger will be the impression you make."

This advice holds true for the writer of memoir. Immerse yourself in the past, yes, but never lose sight of the present. Find the strategies that will allow you to hold both open for the reader.

Into the Fire

I just got back from teaching at *The Sun* magazine's three-day writing retreat in Rowe, Massachusetts. The retreat is called "Into the Fire: *The Sun* Celebrates Personal Writing." In all my sessions, but particularly in the last one that I offered on Saturday night, I invited participants to walk into that fire to see what they might find. The title of this session was "Who Are You?" My objective was to make the participants aware of what they could gain in a piece of personal writing by paying attention to the multiple selves that were in conversation on the page. By investigating our experiences from a number of vantage points and perspectives, we create more rounded characters of ourselves, and we also produce a more tonally textured piece of writing as the voices of the various parts of ourselves vibrate against one another.

I want to share the writing prompts that I gave the people who came to my session in case you might find them helpful for your own personal essays.

1. Start by recalling someone from the past who calls up in you a moment of shame, guilt, or regret. Spend about five minutes writing from the prompt "I can't tell you . . . ." The objective is to get down the facts that led to the shame, guilt, or regret.
2. Shift to something from your present-day life that a memory of the past invites into the conversation. Again, spend about five minutes writing from this prompt: "Instead, let me tell you about . . . ."
3. Spend about five minutes writing from the prompt "When I think of the person I was then, I . . . ." The idea here is to look at your past self from the perspective that you have now.

4. Complete these two sentences: "Back then I thought . . ." and "Now I see (or understand) that . . ."

5. Then complete these two sentences, applying them to either the past experience or the present-day one: "Part of me wishes . . ." and "But another part of me . . ."

6. Spend as much time as you need with this final prompt: "If I could rewrite that moment (the one from the past), I'd . . ." and "But I can't. All I can do (or all I have) is . . ."

When I write a personal essay, I usually have a story to tell, and it invites another story, one that I'd rather not tell because it makes me uncomfortable to do so. It's that second story that makes the essay resonate. This exercise will leave you with the fragmented bones of an essay. The sections may not cohere until you flesh them out and rearrange them to create an essay in which past and present merge. The results can be startling. Many of the people who attended my session said afterward that this exercise took them to significantly life-changing and healing moments of clarity. Isn't that exactly what we're after in a good personal essay?

PART 5 ❧ Language

"Not by the Hair of My Chinny Chin Chin"

Language is not an abstract construction of the
learned, or of dictionary-makers, but is
something arising out of the work, needs, ties,
joys, affections, tastes, of long generations
of humanity, and has its bases broad
and low, close to the ground.

—WALT WHITMAN

Words, too, have genuine substance—mass
and weight and specific gravity.

—TIM O'BRIEN

Stylin'

As I mentioned in the introduction to this book, Mavis Gallant, in her brief essay about style in writing, says, "The only question worth asking about a story—or a poem, or a piece of sculpture, or a new concert hall—is, 'Is it dead or alive?'" Within any distinct style (yours might not be mine and vice versa) there are tricks of language to be learned that we can adapt to useful purpose in any style that we use in our own work.

With that in mind I turn to some passages from Ann Beattie's story "In the White Night." This is the story of Vernon and Carol, parents grieving the death of their daughter. The story opens with them leaving a party. Their host calls to them, "Don't think about a cow." This is a carryover from a game they've been playing at the party. "Don't think about an apple," the host says, and of course, Carol, our point of view character, can't get that image out of her head. This is a story about the adjustments we make in order to go on living in our grief. We try to put the images of our losses out of our minds, but of course, we're never fully successful.

Here's a writing activity that involves two passages from Beattie's story and asks you to think about some of her strategies with language and then put them to use in sections from a piece of fiction, creative nonfiction, or poem that you've written or are writing.

The first passage takes place as Vernon and Carol are driving home from the party: "They passed safely through the last intersection before their house. The car didn't skid until they turned onto their street. Carol's heart thumped hard, once, in the second when she felt the car becoming light, but they came out of the skid easily."

Here we have a passage that begins with two declarative sentences that state the safe passage of the car though the last intersection before home. Those sentences put a steady sound into our heads. Then we're surprised with a new sound that comes from a variation in sentence structure in the third sentence, which contains the moment of the car's slide and Carol's response to it. The sentence thumps us the way "Carol's heart thumped hard, once." Notice the choice of the verb, *thumped*, with its *th*, its *mp*, its *d*. This is a word that bangs its way onto the page. Notice, too, the caesura that Beattie creates with the word *once*, set off with commas, that pause, while the car is skidding. Finally, notice how the subordinate clause, with its subject and verb echoing the declarative sentences that began the passage, returns us to steady ground once the danger has passed. The sentence structure in this passage expresses the emotional content of the action being described.

Writing Prompt #1

Find a passage in your draft that describes an action. Use sentence variety to express the emotional content of the moment.

The second passage comes just as Carol and Vernon are leaving the party and are making their way to their car. "In the small, bright areas under the streetlights, there seemed for a second to be some logic to all the swirling snow. If time itself could only freeze, the snowflakes could become the lacy filigree of a valentine." The first part of the sentence, "In the small, bright areas under the streetlights," strings two adjectives together in spite of all the advice we hear about paring down our adjectives and adverbs. Those two stresses slow the sentence down and serve to emphasize the bright areas being presented to the readers. The pace of the sentence forces us to look at what's being described. In the midst of the swirling snow Beattie allows the language to be a little loose, to be expressive of what she's describing. Notice how the sentence opens with a subordinate clause and the rest that comes at its end. It's into this pause that the snow comes. Notice, too, the assonance and consonance, the repetition of the *f* sound in *freeze, snowflakes,* and *filigree;* the rhyming action of *snowflakes* and *lacy* and of *freeze* and *filigree.* Finally, notice how Beattie makes a metaphor from the detail of the snowflakes, saying, "If time could only freeze, the snowflakes could become the lacy filigree of a valentine." In a story about a couple trying to live in the aftermath of their daughter's tragic death from leukemia, this metaphor is not only descriptive but also expressive of the sort of regret that couple experiences while at the same time making the adjustments necessary to their comfort.

Writing Prompt #2

Find a passage in your fiction, nonfiction, or poem that you think could better express what you've come to the page to explore. Write one sentence that uses successive stresses, or any other means, to slow the pace and call attention to a detail or a description. Then write another sentence in which you construct a metaphor from a detail, a metaphor that becomes a container for the emotional center of the story.

Richard Ford, when asked in a *Paris Review* interview about the single aspect of fiction that was central to his writing process, stressed the importance of language: "I'm always interested in *words,* and no matter what I'm doing—describing a character or a landscape or writing a line of dialogue—I'm moved, though not utterly commanded by an interest in the sound and rhythm of the words, in addition, I ought to say, to what the words actually denote." Ford rightly points out that the music of language isn't solely the province of poets. Language, even in prose, is always directly connected to the expression of meaning.

The Value of a Beautiful Sentence

Ellen Gilchrist's short story "A Love Story" is exactly what it says it is, the story of a man and woman coming together in old age. Here are the last four sentences of the story: "Love is redeemable. You get your money back from love and you get to keep it, too. I think. I hope and pray."

Notice the confidence of the first declarative sentence and the second as well. The story leans toward this uplifting ending. A short statement followed by a longer one and then another short statement that pulls us up . . . well, it pulls us up short. "I think," the narrator says, and suddenly the story that seemed to be heading in one direction starts turning back on itself. The pace of the passage grinds to a halt: *I think*. Period. Big pause, or a caesura if you will—a rest in which we hear the narrator mulling over her initial confident observations. Then the narrator goes on to the last sentence: "I hope and pray." The last sentence tries to turn the story back to its initial target, that strong statement on the value and steadfastness of love, only now, because of the sentence structure and what it creates, any sort of certainty is impossible, and we're left with a commingling of the hope that love is redeemable and the possibility that it's not.

Uncertainty is a good thing at the end of a narrative. A simultaneous gain and loss captures the complexity of human existence. The way one sentence follows another, if we pay attention to syntax and rhythm, should express the final effect we want the narrative to have on a reader. Try taking a passage in something you've written, or are writing, that seems wooden to you. Think about the effect you're trying to create. Play around with sentence variety or syntax to see if lengthening, shortening, or rearranging can unlock this passage and make it seem alive to you.

The *Columbus Dispatch* recently ran a feature on the area's scholar-athletes who are about to graduate from high school. They all responded to a series of interview questions. I took particular notice of the question that asked them to name their least favorite class. More than a few said that English was their least favorite because "writing essays is hard." This started me thinking about why well-crafted sentences can turn my head in a heartbeat and make me fall in love with the arrangement of words on the page.

Take this passage from *The Great Gatsby*, for example, that describes Nick Carraway's first glimpse of his cousin Daisy and her friend Jordan Baker:

> The only completely stationary object in the room was an enormous couch on which two young women were buoyed up as though upon an anchored balloon. They were both in white, and their dresses were rippling and fluttering as if they had just been blown back in after a short flight around the house. I must have stood for a few moments listening to the whip and snap of the curtains and the groan of a picture on a wall. Then there was a boom as Tom Buchanan shut the rear windows and the caught wind died out about the room, and the curtains and the rugs and the two young women ballooned slowly to the floor.

There's a good deal of action in those sentences even though most of them are describing the stationary Daisy and Jordan. The "rippling and fluttering" dresses, the "whip and snap of the curtains," "the groan of a picture on a wall," and finally, the boom from Tom shutting the windows, the only concrete action in the passage and one that literally takes the air out of the room. Notice the progressive tense of "rippling and fluttering" to give a sense of an ongoing motion, the hard p sounds at the end of "whip and snap" to evoke the sharp sounds of the curtains being blown by a hard wind. Finally, notice the compounds in the last sentence, each *and*, the way slowing the sentence down as "the two young women ballooned slowly to the floor." Such a vivid portrait made possible by the intricacies of language.

Or this passage from Nick as he opens the book: "When I came back from the East last autumn I felt that I wanted the world to be in uniform and at a sort of moral attention forever; I wanted no more riotous excursions with privileged glimpses into the human heart. Only Gatsby, the man who gives his name to this book, was exempt from my reaction—Gatsby, who represented everything for which I have an unaffected scorn." Here we have a more abstract passage meant to make plain Nick's state of mind on the other side of the events he's about to describe, but even here in less precisely detailed sentences, Fitzgerald uses a metaphor—the world in uniform and standing "at some sort of moral attention"—to stylize, or literally dress up, Nick's reaction to this portion of his life. "I wanted no more riotous excursions with privileged glimpses into the human heart." Notice the use of assonance—the repetition of the *s* sounds in *riotous, excursions, glimpses*. Also notice the alliteration of *human heart*. This stylized language gives what could have been a rather plain sentence more sizzle. Finally, notice the parallel structures in the last sentence that occur each time the name Gatsby is used and then amplified by first an appositive ("the man who gives his name to this book") and then an adjectival clause ("who represented everything for which I have an unaffected scorn"). This parallelism, along with the repetition of the name, emphasizes Nick's strong feelings for Gatsby. So, a passage whose primary purpose is to give us information also has music at its heart.

It's that music that we need, not just for the sake of the writing but for our own sakes as well. So much of the world around us is chaotic and without reason. A well-crafted sentence is an antidote against this discord. A precise and beautifully constructed sentence holds the chaos of our lives at bay. It provides a structure that gives us the illusion that we can live forever even if our words are describing the moments that threaten to destroy us.

Some of those scholar-athletes didn't like English class because they found it hard to write essays. Sure, it's hard to write a beautiful sentence, and I'll admit it's harder for some than for others. Still, there's something about a gorgeous sentence that makes me feel all is right in the world even if it isn't. I labor nearly every day of my life to write such sentences. I gladly take on this work because it's the only way I know to give some sort of integrity to the world around me. It's the only way I know—at least for the time I spend immersed in word choice and syntax and structure—to shape the life I'm living, to rely on the music of language. Why shouldn't writing a good and beautiful sentence be hard? It's our attempt at salvation.

The Art of the Twerk

Writing the Miley Cyrus Way

To start . . . ahem . . . with a sentence I never in my wildest dreams could have imagined writing: Miley Cyrus has something to teach us about writing. Intrigued? Read on. Shaking your head in disbelief? Wondering about my sanity? Stick with me. I'm thinking about the outlandish. I'm thinking about encouraging outrageous personae as a way of opening up aspects of our material that otherwise might remain closed. How can we use exaggeration to give some jazz to lifeless prose? It's time to consider the art of the twerk.

Let's start by admitting that we all have a number of different aspects to our personalities. We may be a sober, studious bookworm, but given the right circumstances, we may also be a fun-loving imp who loves to play practical jokes or the smooth-talking con artist who will say whatever needs to be said to get what he or she wants. We may be Arnold Friend from Joyce Carol Oates's story "Where Are You Going? Where Have You Been?" ("Gonna get you, baby"). Or Dill Harris from Harper Lee's *To Kill a Mockingbird* ("I've been up since four. I always get up at four. My daddy was a railroad man"). Or Daisy Buchanan from F. Scott Fitzgerald's *The Great Gatsby* ("It makes me sad because I've never seen such—such beautiful shirts before"). Sometimes we forget that these aspects of our personalities come into play when we're writing, whether we're writing poetry or prose. Sometimes, when our words on the page lack a certain something (energy, urgency, tone), we need to call up one or more of our personae to make the writing vibrant and resonant.

So, here's an exercise designed for injecting life into wooden language:

1. Write down a few of your personae, the more conflicting the better.

2. Take a few lines from something you're working on that feel wooden to you or a section that hasn't quite announced its reason for being included in what you're writing. Or write a few lines of ugly prose. What makes it ugly? Maybe passive voice constructions, vague or trite language, mixed metaphors, a neutral tone. Maybe it ends up something like this: "A boat was on the water. It wasn't moving with the current. It was pushed back. It kept ending up where it started."

    You probably recognize this as an uglified form of the haunting final line of *The Great Gatsby*. You can work with that if you wish, or you can take a favorite passage from poetry or prose and ugly it up. Take the life and beauty and emotion right out of it.

3. Choose two of your personae that seem to be incompatible and rewrite your passage twice, each time exaggerating a different aspect of your personality to see what you might discover.

Sometimes we need to greatly exaggerate something in order to shock the language. Once the language has a life, it starts to reveal. What it reveals may surprise us. We may find ourselves more closely connected to the words we're putting on the page. We may discover an urgency that we lacked. We may feel a door open to somewhere we didn't know we needed to go. We may sense a meaning and a purpose we didn't previously know. All sorts of things can happen if the language is alive. One way to make it so is to really exaggerate some aspect of the self. Sometimes to make our writing work, we have to make it twerk.

Communal and Personal Voices

A few years ago Dinty Moore asked me to contribute something to *The Rose Metal Press Field Guide to Writing Flash Nonfiction.* I don't recall why, but at the time Dinty asked me for a contribution, I was pondering issues of voice, possibly because flash nonfiction is often voice driven, or at least it is for me.

I remember one of my writing teachers, Gerald Shapiro, saying that he thought a good writer was usually a good mimic. I've always thought that a writer's voice comes in part from the voices that surrounded him or her in childhood, a chorus of voices rising up from various communities—town, neighborhood, church, family—and in part from the individual speaking either in concert with those communal voices or in resistance to them.

Ancient Greek drama becomes an interesting way of thinking about how this works. In those plays a chorus provided a cultural backdrop from which a single actor spoke. The voice of that actor was more personal, more lyric, giving the drama a more textured sound of an individual speaking from and being considered by a community.

Being aware of the communal and the personal voice when we write flash nonfiction can create a more textured sound. It can also lend a note of urgency, particularly if the juxtaposition of communal and individual creates a tension in the speaker. This tension pushes the piece along as the different voices rub together, providing the conflict of sensibilities crucial to the quick exploration of subject matter and character.

Here's a writing activity that will help you practice this dance between the communal and the personal voices. Allow yourself no more than 750 words.

1. Recall a saying from one of your communities (e.g., family, church, school, scout troop, neighborhood, town) and write an opening line that contains that saying.
2. Keep writing using the language of the community to introduce a character. Here's an example from the opening of my essay "Dumber Than": "A box of rocks. That boy—oh you know the one."
3. Put that character in action. Again, an example from "Dumber Than": "Dropped his cat from that second-story sleeping porch just to see if it was true, what they said about cats always landing on their feet."
4. Find a place to step forward and to speak more personally. Extend the narrative or create a new scene: "Once at Halloween, I caught him soaping the windshield of my '73 Plymouth Duster."
5. As you turn toward the end of your essay, consider how the persona you've established for yourself is fitting into, or separating itself from, the persona of the group. Be aware of any tensions that exist between the different aspects of yourself and how what you're writing invites you to do a quick exploration of your own character.
6. At the very end find a way to blend your personal voice with the communal voice of the group: "That's when we got all righteous. Don't act like it's not true. Dumber than a bagful of hammers, we said. Now that's one thing we always knew for sure."

Voice in Creative Nonfiction

My friend Sue William Silverman has an article that discusses the importance of voice in creative nonfiction. Borrowing from William Blake, she defines the two major voices that writers use in memoirs and personal essays as the Song (or Voice) of Innocence and the Song (or Voice) of Experience. The first, Sue says, "relates the facts of the experience, the surface subject." This is the voice of narration, telling us what happened in what order. This voice, in its purest form, can know only what the innocent "you" knew at the time of the events. The Voice of Experience, on the other hand, knows much, much more from its wiser position of distance from the events. This voice is the more reflective voice, the voice that interprets the subject matter and guides the reader through the experience that's being dramatized.

Sue uses an example from her second memoir, *Love Sick: One Woman's Journey through Sexual Addiction*, to illustrate how the two voices can intertwine. In this section of her memoir she's recalling her experience as a college freshman with an older, married lover via a scarf that he gave her: "I press the scarf against my nose and mouth. I take a deep breath. The scent is of him— leaves smoldering in autumn dusk—and I believe it is a scent I have always craved, one I will always want. I don't understand why the scent of the scarf . . . seems more knowable, more tangible than the rest of him."

Sue's passage, as she points out in the article, begins with the Voice of Experience romanticizing the man and the scarf, before "moving into a more sober persona, the Voice of Experience, which reveals that the scarf is a metaphor for alienation, loneliness, loss. This sober, experienced voice, in other words, guides the reader through the quagmire of the addiction." Sue goes on to point out that the texture of the Voice of Innocence blending with the Voice of Experience allows the writer to deepen his or her own character. She advocates using these voices to form a cohesive chord. "For without these varied voices," she argues, "what you have, basically, is a one-note voice telling a one-note story."

With the objective of forming that cohesive chord, Sue comes up with five "notes" that can move the you as character from Innocence to Experience.

Which leads me to a writing exercise. I asked the MFA students in my creative nonfiction workshop to come up with prompts for an exercise that would allow people to put Sue's five notes into practice. So, with apologies to Sue for blending our voices with hers, here's what we came up with. I'll first quote the notes as Sue has described them, and then I'll insert the writing prompts that my students devised.

Before getting to Sue's notes, I'd ask everyone to think of an object that they associate with a guilty feeling from childhood. Perhaps it's the candy bar you stole or the toy that you whined and whined for and then promptly lost or broke. Anything concrete that gives you a guilty feeling now when you think of it.

Sue's Note 1: "An impersonal, factual persona is an element of the Song of Innocence and provides straightforward exposition to let the reader know where you are in time and place."

Writing Prompt: Writing in the present tense, begin with a line something like, "I am [fill in the blank] years old, and I'm [fill in the blank by considering place, time, the object, other characters]. Your objective is to set the scene by utilizing only the Voice of Innocence.

Sue's Note 2: "An observant but still slightly distant persona that introduces a more writerly style, yet is still part of the Song of Innocence. Here, you provide the reader with an idea of how you observe your world of the senses."

Writing Prompt: Begin a sentence with, "I see [or smell, taste, hear, feel], and then fill in the blank with a combination of sensory details. If you can use more than one sense, all the better. Concentrate on the object in the way that Sue focused on the scarf in her example.

Sue's Note 3: "A more evolved persona, one with feelings, hovering between the Song of Innocence and the Song of Experience. You're writing closer to the heart, with a sense of urgency and raw emotion . . . here you will explore how you felt when the events originally occurred. In other words, you're feeling the facts of the story."

Writing Prompt: Begin a sentence with, "It [the object] makes me think of [fill in the blank], and I believe [fill in the blank]. Here we're trying to articulate something you felt or believed at the time of the event, a feeling or thought that's probably evolved over time.

Sue's Note 4: "By introducing a metaphoric persona, you bring the reader into the Song of Experience. This metaphoric voice beings to offer insight into the facts and feelings."

Writing Prompt: Use your object to construct a metaphor. "The [object] is [fill in the blank]. Construct more than one metaphor if you wish. Let the metaphors contain your emotional response to the event and the object and the feeling of guilt that you still carry with you.

Sue's Note 5: "This fully developed, reflective character (Song of Experience) culminates with all the notes. Metaphor is deepened in order to connect each element and event in the work into a cohesive whole. You reflect and ruminate upon the past, consider others in your life. What do you hope, wish, dream, fear? What are the lessons you've learned?"

Writing Prompt: Write a sentence of action involving you and the object. Then complete this sentence: "I didn't know that . . . ." And this one, "When I think of the boy/girl I was then, I . . . ."

This exercise should add texture to your voice and also invite the various parts of yourself to converse about the subject at hand. The result should be a deepening of the material.

Personae and Tone in Fiction

I'm still thinking about this issue of persona and how it contributes to the life of our prose. Part of the pleasure of reading a memoir comes from the resonance of different layers (or personae, if you will) of the narrator vibrating against one another. Does the same hold true for fiction? If we look at a third-person narrative, will we find shifts in persona of the effaced narrator and modulations of tone used to good effect?

I start with Raymond Carver's story "A Small, Good Thing," about the death of a little boy and what his grieving parents find in the presence of a baker whom they once considered a menace. Here's a paragraph from the opening of the story when the mother, Ann Weiss, comes to the bakery to order a birthday cake for her son, Scotty:

> She gave the baker her name, Ann Weiss, and her telephone number. The cake would be ready on Monday morning, just out of the oven, in plenty of time for the child's party that afternoon. The baker was not jolly. There were no pleasantries between them, just the minimum exchange of words, the necessary information. He made her feel uncomfortable, and she didn't like that. While he was bent over the counter with the pencil in his hand, she studied his coarse features and wondered if he'd ever done anything else with his life besides be a baker. She was a mother and thirty-three years old, and it seemed to her that everyone, especially someone the baker's age—a man old enough to be her father—must have children who'd gone through this special time of cakes and birthday parties. There must be that between them, she thought. But he was abrupt with her—not rude,

just abrupt. She gave up trying to make friends with him. She looked into the back of the bakery and could see a long, heavy wooden table with aluminum pie pans stacked at one end; and beside the table a metal container filled with empty racks. There was an enormous oven. A radio was playing country-western music.

The story establishes an initial persona as the voice of the effaced narrator blends with the consciousness of Mrs. Weiss. I'd describe the persona as being guarded, observant, restrained, a little prickly. The prose reflects that with its simple, declarative sentences. Language and sentence structure and tone work together to express the state of mind of Mrs. Weiss as she deals with this baker two days before the accident that will cost her son his life.

Mrs. Weiss, of course, is about to live through a series of events that will require much more from the prose than this initial persona can provide. Consider, then, the final paragraph of the story. Scotty has died, and Mrs. and Mr. Weiss have received a series of brusque and seemingly menacing phone calls from the baker about picking up the birthday cake: "Your Scotty, I got him ready for you," the man's voice said. "Did you forget him?" Finally, Mr. and Mrs. Weiss figure out that the calls are coming from the baker, and they drive down there to confront him. After their burst of anger, the baker invites them to sit. He apologizes. He gives them his sympathy. He explains that he's a baker, that he has no children of his own, that he knows loneliness. Then he offers them bread: "'Smell this,' the baker said, breaking open a dark loaf. 'It's a heavy bread, but rich.' They smelled it, then he had them taste it. It had the taste of molasses and coarse grains. They listened to him. They ate what they could. They swallowed the dark bread. It was like daylight under the fluorescent trays of light. They talked on into the early morning, the high, pale cast of light in the windows, and they did not think of leaving."

Notice the difference in sound between the two passages from Carver's story. It seems to me that even though the sentences are perhaps even terser here, they make a very different sound, one I'd describe as quieter, reverential, humble, full of forgiveness. It's the surprising moment of grace found from an unexpected source upon which the story depends for its effect. The resonance comes from the shift in the persona that allows the sound of this passage to vibrate against the sounds of other personae at work in the story.

We often remember a moment in a piece of fiction in part because of the way the sound of the prose surprises us. In a first-person novel or short story, we, of course, have at our disposal the various aspects of the narrator's personality to create these shifts in persona and sound. What I hope the Carver example illustrates is that even in a third-person narrative aspects of the main characters' personalities merge with the sound of the effaced narrator's voice—that disembodied storytelling voice—thereby deepening the experience of the novel or story.

Just as we need to be aware of our own multiple personae when writing memoir, we need to pay attention to our fictional characters and how they're slightly different people in each moment of a narrative. In both memoir and fiction we sometimes have to consciously exaggerate a dimension of persona in order to fully express a shift in the narrative, one that will stay with the reader far beyond the reading.

Paying Attention to Form in Flash Nonfiction

Brenda Miller writes about how paying attention to form in creative nonfiction can invite the writer to make "inadvertent revelations where the writer no longer seems in complete control." She says, "Form essentially becomes the writer's inky courage." Here, then, is a writing activity I developed that asks the writer to work with metaphor as a way of coming at emotional material indirectly. If it works, the activity should make the following outcome possible (again, quoting Brenda): "Revelation or discovery emerges organically from the writing; the essay now seems to reveal information about the writer rather than the writer revealing these tidbits directly to the reader." Sometimes our material is too emotional for us to face head-on. Sometimes we need a form in which to contain it. By paying attention to the artistry, we can discover what we have to say. Here, then, are the steps of the activity, followed by the essay I wrote in response to the prompts.

1. Choose an abstraction to write about, something large and intense like grief or sorrow or love or joy.
2. Daydream a list of particular emotional memories that the abstraction calls up in you. Write a paragraph focusing on one of those memories. Begin with the line "I remember . . . ."
3. Now do a bit more daydreaming. When you think of the moment you've portrayed in the first paragraph, what other memories come to you? Grab onto one of them and make that the focus of your second paragraph, moving forward or backward in time.
4. In the third paragraph concentrate on a particular object

that comes from one of your memories. This object will be the title of your 750-or-fewer word essay. Describe the object. Put it into action. Gather the details that will lead to your final paragraph.

5. In this last paragraph let the object grow into a metaphor for the intense emotional meaning rising in the essay. Write a simile, such as "That sloth is as slow as grief" (from Jill Christman's "The Sloth," a much better example than my own essay).

6. Find a fact with which to open the essay. Add a sentence to the beginning. Find a way to evoke that fact at the end.

The Kite

A buoyant object floats in the air without using energy. It goes as it goes. I remember an afternoon in April—this was forty years ago—when I drove home with the sort of carefree delight that an eighteen-year-old boy can have in spring. My parents were waiting for me, and had been for some time, but I didn't know it. My father said, "Where have you been?" My mother's face was set with what I now know was worry. I was to drive them to the hospital, she said. My father had been ill in a way that I took little note of, and now the doctor was admitting him for tests. It was my Easter vacation from school, and I'd been at the state park with some friends. We'd been flying kites, and I had no reason to think that my parents might be in need of me. A sunny day, a cloudless sky, daffodils in bloom, the smell of grass, a fresh wind—I thought I had all the time in the world. But when my mother said, "We went out looking for you," I knew that I was wrong. Standing in my house, I felt cut loose from all that was familiar and safe, swept up in time's irrepressible current, and yet anchored to all that was yet to come.

Days later, in the parking lot of the hospital, my mother told me, "Your dad has cancer." Just like that, something inside broke free and left me forever.

I've never forgotten the way I held onto the string as overhead the kite tugged at me. I bent back my head and watched it flit and dip and soar. I heard the plastic shudder and pop on its balsa wood sticks. I felt each change of direction, the kite going slack or taut.

Now I think of quail and goldfinches and the way they bob and dip. Swallows swoop and arc. All according to their instincts for flight. All in a beautiful and graceful motion. But this kite,

167

glorious as it was, shook with the wind, rose and fell in a ragged and unpredictable way. No fault of its own. It was plastic and light wood at the mercy of the air currents. I did my best to hold it steady. I felt the strain of it trying to keep itself aloft. I thought, *This kite is as stupid as misery.* How easy it would have been to open my hand and let it go. In the end I couldn't save my father, nor can I save myself or anyone I love. Still, that day, only a length of string between me and the sky, I kept faith. I believed in the miracle of flight. I held on.

The Thing Said

Ten Thoughts on Writing Dialogue in Memoir

1. Accept the fact that you'll never remember exactly what someone said. Trust me. You may think you will, but you won't. The thing said is lost to time; all that remains is the shape you give it as you do your best to call it back.

2. Other people will remember the thing said slightly differently than you will remember it. Let them. It may help in the composing process to hear what they remember. They may give you a line better than any you could have written. If it has the ring of truth, go with it. If it doesn't have the ring of truth, put it away from you.

3. The ring of truth is the feeling memoir writers get when something flips over inside them and they know they're in touch with the essence of the experience they're trying to re-create on the page. Dialogue can take us to the ring of truth. Maybe a father said, as mine did, "Can't never did nothing." When did he say it? Often. I may not remember the exact moments when he said that line, but I can recall the feeling of inadequacy it always gave me, the feeling that I'd never be able to please him.

4. What were the things the people in your memoir said with frequency? Those lines are always there for you to use—yes, even if you don't remember if they said them at the exact time you hear them saying them in the scenes you're writing.

5. Dialogue should be distinctive. Read enough fiction to catch onto the fact that the reader should be able to

identify the speaker without any dialogue attribution simply from the sound of the voice.

6. Cadence, vocabulary, syntax. Mine isn't yours, and yours isn't mine.

7. Dialogue should move the narrative forward while also contributing to characterization. In Barry Lopez's "Murder" the author recalls the time a woman, a stranger, asked him to kill her husband. "I've got a gun over there in that car," she says. "He's in a garage outside of town, working on his car. All you have to do is walk in there, walk right up to him, and shoot him. He won't know you. There's no one else there. No one could hear." This speech lays out the plan, but it also reveals just how desperate this woman is and how intensely she's imagined this solution to her problem.

8. Dialogue has subtext. Everything we say doesn't say everything we want to say. A well-constructed line of dialogue can be interesting for what it doesn't say. In my essay "Drunk Man" I recall the time my father offered to buy a local man with a drinking problem a meal. "C'mon, Odie," he said. "Let's get you something to eat." Odie picked up right away on the thing not said and the judgment it carried. "I don't need no handout. Let me out of this damn truck."

9. Miscommunication through dialogue can make a memorable scene. What have you or the people in your life said that was misunderstood, that caused some shift in your relationships?

10. Spoken speech isn't written speech. Even memoirs require a little shaping when it comes to dialogue. Sometimes we have someone say a line (something we "remember" them saying) even if we're not sure he or she said it at that exact time. Sometimes we give the line a little something extra by combining things we remember someone saying. Maybe we let a character use a pet name that

he or she always had for us. Maybe we make the speech a little less or a little more formal than it might have been. Maybe we take liberties in service of the work a particular scene is trying to do. Maybe we mess things up a bit. Everyday speech usually isn't without a little mess. We do what we can to convince our readers that our characters said what we say they did even if they really didn't. Sometimes we rearrange, add, and subtract. We remember that our dialogue has to have the feel of reality, and sometimes to do that, we give ourselves permission to make stuff up—not to the point that we change the essence of who someone was or the experience that we're recalling. We don't lie. We shape. There, I've said it.

Alligators and Marshmallows

A Lesson in Humor

My cousin likes to tell the story of the time when she was a girl, about ten years old, and she was on vacation on Sanibel Island with her parents. They went to a gator farm, and there she was given a stick with a marshmallow on the end and told to hold it out to an alligator and the alligator would come and take the marshmallow from the end of the stick.

I've seen the photographs. I've seen my cousin crouching at the water's edge, holding out the stick, less than three feet away from an alligator, just waiting for him to snap up the marshmallow.

This is a story that holds all there is to hold about my cousin's complicated relationship with her parents. This is a story fraught with tension, the sort that comes from no one understanding the danger that the little girl is in—has been put in by her parents, who believe this is an experience she'll never forget.

And they're right—she never has. When she tells the story, she plays it for a joke. She points out that her father told her to hold still so he could get a good picture. I've even seen a photograph that someone else took, and there's my uncle crouching a few feet behind my cousin, his camera to his eye. "Hold it," I imagine him saying. "Hold still. I want to get the right angle for this shot." We get a great laugh out of this story, but I know the pain behind the humor. My cousin doesn't acknowledge it when she tells the story, but I can feel it in the facts. A sweet little girl put in harm's way by parents who wanted her to experience feeding a marshmallow to an alligator. What the photos don't tell you is that my cousin could never quite please my aunt and uncle. She strived to do so. She does to this day, even though she knows she'll never succeed. Imagine her as that little girl, bravely facing that gator, making her offering, eager to do what her parents asked of her.

Once, when she told the story, she said, "I don't know why they didn't give me a longer stick."

My aunt, with impeccable timing and a wit so sharp it cut, said, "Well, you couldn't have handled a longer stick."

We roared with laughter at that because it was a line that was so insistent at avoiding the real issue while at the same time proving the pain that lies at the heart of the story.

There's a lesson about humor in all of this. The human condition is funny when the people in the midst of the story aren't aware of the humor and don't call attention to the pain it's masking. The details do the work. "Well, you couldn't have handled a longer stick," my aunt said, and we laughed and laughed at the thought that she and my uncle, in the process of looking out for my cousin by not giving her a longer stick, justified what they were doing and ignored the danger of it. The ironic tension between what's said and what's not gives this line a humor counterweighted with gravity. My aunt's words make me laugh while at the same time they make me cringe.

My cousin keeps these photos on her refrigerator. She looks at them every day. She says to me, and she's dead serious when she does, "I look at them, and I think how lucky I am to be alive."

Comedy in Fiction

When I was in the first grade, my class took a field trip to Santa Claus Land, an amusement park in southwestern Indiana. My mother gave me a quarter in case I had need of it. Maybe I'm thinking about this because it's Mother's Day or maybe because this happened in May, when it was hotter than it should have been and at a time when there was no air conditioning in our school bus. The point being that on the drive home, everyone was extremely thirsty. Parched, I guess you could say.

What a blessing it was, then, to find a roadside café open for business with cold bottles of pop for sale. I remember sitting at the counter on a stool that swiveled and asking the waitress how much a bottle cost.

"A dime," she said.

My heart sank. "I don't have a dime," I told her, and she was kind enough to bring me a free glass of ice water, which I drank while watching my friends guzzle Pepsi, Coke, orange Nehi, 7UP.

When I got home and told my mother this story, she asked me why I hadn't used my quarter to buy a bottle of pop.

"Because it wasn't a dime," I said. "I had to have a dime."

"Son," she said, "it's time we had a talk about change."

Now, when I look back on the boy I was, I find myself laughing at his ignorance. Then, in a tick, the laughter always dissolves, and I look a little closer, and I find myself wishing I could tell that kid what a quarter is. "You could have had a bottle of pop," I want to say. "Heck, you could've had two bottles!"

That's when I remember that glass of ice water. Even though I was glad for it on that hot day, I also felt how it marked me as the kid who didn't have enough money to buy a bottle of pop. As I look back on that first grader, drinking ice water and wanting so badly to have what his friends were having, I start to feel the yearning underneath the comedy. I start to feel the wanting and its frustration, which makes me a little sad, and that's another important element of the comic in fiction. The funny and the sad are often contained within the same character, the same event.

I also think of my mother and how she'd never planned to have a child. Things happened, though, and I was born when she was forty-five. Nearly twice the age of my friends' parents, she must have been sensitive to any imperfections in her own maternal skills. She was a grade school teacher. She taught kids about change all the time. How could it be that the lesson had never made its way to me? I also think about how my mother was such a timid woman. I inherited her shyness. I didn't like standing out from the crowd the way I did that afternoon in the café. When my mother said we'd have to have a talk about change, I felt her own embarrassment.

On the surface this is an amusing family anecdote that gets told for years and years, and everyone laughs. Beneath the surface, though, lies a more human story of a shy kid, an unused quarter, a desperate want, a deep embarrassment shared with his mother.

I'll never forget that my mother and I were alone in our house that day. She poured Pepsi over ice in an aluminum drinking glass, and I sipped the foam the way I liked to do, and then I drank and drank while she got some coins from her purse—pennies, nickels, dimes, quarters—and started to teach me what was what. Each coin contained a certain number of the others. My quarter was made up of twenty-five pennies, five nickels, two dimes and a nickel. A whole was made up of its parts, just the way characters are in fiction.

A drowsy late afternoon in our farmhouse. My mother and I, connected somewhere deeper than anecdote because of what we shared: the wanting, the embarrassment. The context of our story—that timid kid who wanted a cold bottle of pop, my late-in-life mother who wanted to prove that she could indeed be a good mother at her age—gives the amusing story its weight and makes it something I can't forget. Comedy in fiction should never exist for the sake of the joke alone. It should have something to show us about the human condition. It can be truly memorable if the writer doesn't neglect the human beings at the heart of the humor.

PART 6 ❧ Revision

And the Third Little Pig Lived Happily Ever After

Writing and rewriting are a constant search
for what it is one is saying.

—JOHN UPDIKE

I don't write easily or rapidly. My first draft
usually has only a few elements worth
keeping. I have to find what those are and
build from them and throw out what doesn't
work, or what simply is not alive.

—SUSAN SONTAG

Taking Flight

First Drafts

A wild turkey crossed the road in front of me this morning, and as I slowed, it started to run through the grass—running, running, running, in a most unseemly fashion before spreading its wings, lifting into the air, and taking flight.

Starting a piece of writing is sometimes that way for me. I feel like I'm running and running but nothing is lifting up from the page. I often have plenty of forward momentum in a first draft, but I also have the sense that things haven't really started and I'm waiting for that feeling of liftoff. It's a matter of sensing that I don't really know what the piece is about. I don't know what it is that I've come to the page to explore. Over the years I've come to accept that it's okay to know very little when I begin. I've learned to trust that the writing itself will show me what's important.

A first draft is a draft of discovery. In that draft it's probably better to know very little so we can be open to where the writing takes us. The draft is always smarter than we are. It schools us. It shows us what matters. If we're open to the instruction, our subsequent drafts will take flight. We need to understand that the only thing that matters in a first draft is that we're putting words on the page, lots of them. Let the piece goes where it wants to go. We can shape it after we know what it is.

Felt Sense

Focusing on Revision

Often the thing we've come to say in an essay hovers just at the periphery of our first drafts and in us as well. There are places in those drafts where we can almost bring our most important thoughts to full articulation via reflection, narration, or the artful arrangement of images. Subsequent drafts are usually necessary to more fully integrate what we carry inside us with what we say on the page.

Beginning in 1953, the psychotherapist Eugene Gendlin spent fifteen years analyzing what made psychotherapy successful. His conclusion was that success depended on how well the patient was able to focus on a subtle and vague internal awareness during therapy. Gendlin called this internal awareness "felt sense." Sondra Perl's book of the same name locates felt sense within the field of composition studies in an attempt to better understand what happens in a successful composing process. I'm interested in how this might also be useful in the revision process.

So, here's an exercise that borrows from Perl, with certain subtractions and additions. It's my hope that the exercise will be a means of discovery for writers who want to find deeper emotional and intellectual connections to the hearts of the drafts that they've written. The exercise is designed to help us say more, think more, and feel more as we connect our drafts to what we carry inside us.

1. Identify a place in your draft that makes you feel uncomfortable or a place that seems too vague but also important. Spend some time writing from this prompt: "I don't

want to say anything more about this because if I do . . ." Your objective here is to articulate the fears that keep you from fully exploring your material.

2. From your response to prompt #1, admit what attracts you. What have you said that you can't look away from? Begin writing with the prompt "I know intimately . . ." Don't stop writing for whatever period of time you'd like to set for yourself. There are no rules to how you might approach this step. Images, lists, stream of consciousness writing, notes to yourself—whatever keeps your pen moving and keeps you moving more deeply into your material.

3. Stop writing and give these questions some thought: What makes this material interesting to me? What's the heart of the material? What's important about the material that I haven't yet explored? Wait quietly for a word, image, or phrase to arise from your felt sense of the topic. Write whatever comes.

4. Now step back and think about what you've written. Ask yourself what it's all about. Describe the feeling that you get when you think about it. Where in your body is this feeling centered? Write about what you're feeling inside you right now as you continue to write. Ask yourself whether you're getting closer to what you really want to say. See if you feel yourself getting closer. See if you feel something click into place inside you when you get close and you can tell yourself: "Oh, yes, this is it. This is what I've come to say."

5. If you reach a dead end, ask yourself why the material is so hard for you. Spend a few minutes writing about what's keeping you from writing more deeply into the material.

6. Ask yourself what's missing. What have you yet to get down on paper?

7. Ask yourself where this is leading. Where does the essay want to go?

You should feel free to take liberties with the prompts in order to best suit your revision process. The important thing is to attend to the physical feeling or the image that stands for what you want to say so you can have a genuine sense of what you're trying to get at in your essay. You can then check any passage of the essay against your felt sense to make sure that everything is in service of what first brought you to the page, brought you there before you were aware of why you were writing and before you even had words for what was inside you that made you want to speak. Sometimes we need a revision process that requires us to consider our purpose for writing and to locate that purpose within our visceral reaction to the material.

More Revision Activities

My MFA in Creative Nonfiction Workshop went through some activities last week to help the students with revising their essays. Two of the people in the workshop, Cait Weiss and Jody Gerbig Todd, have been kind enough to allow me to share the activities that they devised. I hope you'll find them as useful as I did. Revision is often a matter of thinking more deeply about our material. Sometimes it's helpful to do that thinking from perspectives we usually wouldn't consider, as in the brainstorming activity that Cait gives us. The deepening of our thinking can also occur, as Jody points out, when we're invited to consider how a particular craft choice such as the white space between sections provides us an opportunity to consider where the tension lies in a piece.

From Cate Weiss

Boardroom brainstorming is not about coming up with a solution, at least not directly. Instead, the experience is about unlocking new, unexpected, often entirely crazy ways of unhinging and reassembling old, worrisome things. Speaking of old, worrisome things: a CNF [creative nonfiction] essay, multiple drafts in, that just won't do what I want it to. Here's one brainstorm strategy teased from corporate America.

The Worst Idea, the Weirdest Idea, and the Idiot Question
1. Write the most painfully obvious "topic sentence," or "thesis," to the essay you're tackling. This is the sentence you want to roll your eyes while uttering, the one that you swear to yourself will never make it into your piece.
2. Write the weirdest, fringe-wild sentence your essay inspires. This is the sentence your inner child / spirit animal / hip-

pie aunt with thirty cats (the one who scarf dances to bongos) might take away as the moral of your story.

3. Write the most obnoxious "What If?" question possible, considering the situations, anxieties, or possibilities your essay discusses. This is the question that aims to be so profound it's absurd or so basic it should go beyond saying.

This exercise might change how you've been looking at things. That's the hope at least. Once you let yourself say the painfully obvious, bizarre, or basic thing, you've incorporated your whole self into the writing process and onto the page, ideally leading to a more cohesive, honest narrative.

If you can, share these sentences with others who have read your work. They might be surprised, and their surprise might help you realize that what you thought was *so obvious, weird,* or *stupid* actually needs further illumination or nurturing in your piece. Or they may just learn your mind's an endless, absurd little trove of surprises. Either way, give it a try and good luck!

From Jody Gerbig Todd
White Space Revision

In our Creative Nonfiction Workshop we assign one another names according to particular skills: Dialogue Diva, Detail Guru, White Space Queen. These names affectionately identify our adeptness in—and our seemingly natural ability to tighten, intensify, and empower—one component of our writing. But many writers also struggle in a particular area, making the process of revision daunting. As you try to revise this weaker area of your manuscript, you might think, as one of my classmates did recently: "I'm in hate with this piece right now. I just sit there, staring at the screen, not knowing what to do with it." We've all been there.

When feeling this way, it might be helpful to use a revision exercise designed specifically for that weakness. Thus (in my attempt to overthrow our current White Space Queen), I have devised five revision exercises to help you think about what happens in the space in between, also known as white space, the double drop, or the section break. Writers can use white space to denote a time jump, a scene change, or a new topic. But that space can become so much more. It can become the silence between notes, the pause between beats, the thing left unsaid—in other words, the tension in your piece.

Here are five exercises, which can be applied to fiction or non-fiction, revision or drafting, in combination or alone. Choose one or several, follow the directions, and see what happens.

1. Give each segment denoted by the double drop, hashtag, or white space a subtitle, including a gerund and a prepositional phrase or its concrete object ("Crying in my Cheerios," e.g., or "Seeing the Shades"). Using gerunds might help you understand your piece's development (even if it's lyrical). If gerunds don't help, try creating other kinds of phrases. Regardless, try to keep the phrases concrete and specific. After you label each section, evaluate whether it shows narrative progression. Does the speaker grow, develop, or realize something in a sequence? Do the subtitles tell you something about the essay's subject matter?

2. (You can try this one as a drafting exercise as well, especially if you've found yourself blocked at the end of a scene.) In each white space write out the following statement and fill in the blanks, or have someone fill them in for you: "You just read about _____, which will reveal _____ about the next part on _____." Try using the first blank's word in the end of the early segment and starting the next section with a sentence using the words in the last two blanks. What happens? (You might find this helpful in combination with #3.)

3. Identify what is at stake in each section. In other words, what does your narrator have to lose? Is it internal/emotional? Is it external/physical? Once you identify these

stakes, make sure that the lines surrounding the white space reveal that tension. (Kate Walbert once taught me that the first line of any novel or story should reveal all the tension contained in the entire story following, so that if a writer is blocked, all he or she must do is to go back to that tension in the first line and write about it in a new way. You might think of the first line after your white space this way.)

4. Find the last image you give in a segment. Imagine you cross off everything after it and end there. What happens to it and the first line of the following segment? Do you land on a powerful and symbolic image that resonates more than the telling of it does? (This might be particularly helpful as a final revision exercise, after you've already figured out and drafted what the piece is centrally about. It also might be particularly helpful for the very last lines of your piece, where writers have a tendency to over-tell.)

5. Take a line highlighted by a workshopper or a line that you feel is meaningful in the piece and move it to before or after a white space. What does that change do for the tension around it? Does it work as a particularly insightful conclusive or introductory statement?

The Doorway between Memoir and Fiction

As someone who writes both fiction and creative nonfiction, I've long been interested in the intersections between the two. More specifically (and this is probably more the teacher in me than the writer), I've been curious about how using both forms to approach the same material can deepen the writer's intellectual and emotional responses. To put it simply, what happens to the revision of a piece of fiction when the writer explores the autobiographical sources that the narrative suggests? Likewise, what happens to a piece of memoir when the writer takes the material and turns it into fiction? I'm interested in the dialogue between the forms and how it affects the revision process.

So, when Dinty Moore proposed a team-taught craft class for the Vermont College of Fine Arts Postgraduate Writers' Conference where we'd both be teaching, I jumped at the chance to work with him. Here, then, is the writing activity that we came up with. Our objective was to explore what happens when we invite an exchange between memoir and fiction.

1. Recall a time when you lied, a time that still makes you feel a little "squirmy" to recall. This shouldn't be a white lie but a lie with lasting consequences. My lie would be one I told when I was in first grade. It may have been the first significant lie I ever told. Our teacher had allowed us to take our sack lunches out on the playground. She warned us to be careful with our milk cartons and not to spill them. Well, of course, I spilled mine. When she asked me what happened, I made up a story about an older boy, someone I'd never seen, coming up the road

(this was a two-room country school) and kicking over my milk and then leaving. I was a good kid. I knew it was wrong to lie. Why had I been so quick to do it? Why does that lie still make me feel uncomfortable when I recall it? When you've identified your lie, write a piece of very brief memoir about it. Try to keep it under 750 words. If you have trouble starting, use the line "I said it happened like this . . ."

2. Now revisit the material of the memoir, only this time use a third-person point of view and give yourself permission to stray from the facts. Invent whatever you wish. In other words, write a brief piece of fiction (again, try to keep it under 750 words). Here's the opening that Dinty suggested for mine: "Tommy's teacher told the class to take their cartons of Dairyville and sack lunches of baloney and cheese on Sunbeam bread out onto the playground that day because the cafeteria still smelled too much like paint. 'Don't spill the milk,' she warned, just as Tommy cleared the doorway to the outside."

3. Has the piece of fiction adjusted your view of the lie that formed the base of the memoir? Dinty suggests that even though the events or dialogue or thoughts that shaped the piece of fiction didn't really happen, "perhaps they suggest some subconscious truth, a deeper layer or view of the real situation." Revise your brief memoir using anything that you learned by writing the piece of fiction.

When I wrote my piece of fiction, I added a character that wasn't there at the time of the actual experience. That character and the way she interacted with the boy, Tommy, ended up showing me that the reason the lie stays with me has something to do with the way I want to see myself and the way I want others to see me. I'm not sure whether I would have gotten to this understanding without transforming my experience into fiction. For me the fiction opened some additional doorways to the memoir and ended up creating a more complicated and textured piece.

To me all writing is thinking with language, and writing in other forms can take our work to a fuller rendering.

Proverbs for Revising a Novel

> Sitting peacefully, doing nothing
> spring comes
> and the grass grows all by itself.
>
> —LAO TZU

I'm nearing the end of the first draft of a new novel. Maybe a scene or two more, and I'll have it. Already, I know what my first revision strategy will be. Put that sucker away. Put it out of my mind. Write that short story I've been meaning to write. Live in a world other than the one of the novel. Forget, forget, forget, so I can finally read the novel with fresh eyes, so I can see clearly and analytically, so it'll seem as if someone else wrote this book, so I'll know what needs to be done.

❧

> The quieter you become,
> the more you are able to hear.
>
> —LAO TZU

I usually know it's time to return to the draft when I find myself thinking about it without meaning to. Maybe I'll be out running and I'll hear one of my characters say something. Maybe it'll be something they wanted to say in the draft but I didn't give them a chance. Or maybe I'll be drifting off to sleep and I'll suddenly see the shape of the book in a way I've not been able to see it before. When the book starts talking to me without my invitation, I know it's close to time for me to read through it, taking notes as I go.

> If your mind is empty, it is always ready for
> anything; it is open to everything. In the
> beginner's mind there are many possibilities,
> in the expert's mind there are few.

—SHUNRYU SUZUKI-ROSHI

Waiting allows me to empty my mind. When I read through my draft, I start with the last chapter, the last scene, just to remind myself of where the narrative finally arrives. Then I go back to the beginning, and as I read, I try to stay open to possibilities that are clearer to me now that I know what my novel is. Bernard Malamud said: "First drafts are for learning what your novel or story is about. Revision is working with that knowledge to enlarge and enhance an idea, to re-form it." Reading through the draft reminds me of what brought me to the material in the first place. It makes the center of the book clear to me, and I'm not just talking about plot here. I'm also talking about how the characters rub together in interesting ways. Most important, I'm talking about the thing in the material that's virtually unknowable, that mystery of the human heart that required my efforts with storytelling to try to know it better.

> No snowflake ever falls in the wrong place.

—TS'AI KEN T'AN

Once I know the novel's heart and the place toward which the narrative is headed, I can think about each chapter and each scene and the work they're doing to contribute to the novel's final moves. I can make sure that things are happening when they're supposed to be happening. I can consider the causal chain of events, brushing away what's too dry and without heft or polishing a particular facet or maybe even creating a new one, until the significance to the whole is clear.

Water which is too pure has no fish.

—TS'AI KEN T'AN

I also read with an eye for conflict. I want to make sure that I've given the tensions between characters thorough dramatization and expression. I keep my eye out for the scenes of conflict that cause the characters' positions to shift. Again, I want to know how these scenes are preparing the way for the novel's end.

Before enlightenment, I chopped wood
    and carried water.
After enlightenment, I chopped wood
    and carried water.

—ZEN PROVERB

Novels are made a word at a time, both in the first draft and in all the drafts that follow. Once I've taken care of issues of character and structure, I want to make sure that the language is in the service of what the novel has come to say. I want to make sure that each sentence works the way it should until I'm certain I've created a voice out of the world of the novel that's true to its experience. When an interviewer for the *Paris Review* asked Bernard Malamud how many drafts of a novel he usually did, he had this to say: "Many more than I call three. Usually the last of the first puts it in place. The second focuses, develops, subtilizes. By the third most of the dross is gone. I work with language. I love the flowers of afterthought." Like Malamud, I love arriving at the place where I know what I need to know. Then I can pay attention to the music the language makes on the page, but to get there, I first have to admit I know nothing. I have to ask the draft to teach me.

PART 7 ❧ The Writing Life

*The Two Little Pigs Now Felt Sorry
for Having Been So Lazy
and Built Their Houses with Bricks*

Write a little every day,
without hope, without despair.

—ISAK DINESEN

Successful writers are not the ones
who write the best sentences. They are the
ones who keep writing. They are the ones who
discover what is most important and strangest
and most pleasurable in themselves, and
keep believing in the value of their
work, despite the difficulties.

—BONNIE FRIEDMAN

My Mother's Gifts to Me

Running through the neighborhood this morning, I came upon a young mother playing roller hockey with her two sons at the end of their court. She wasn't just going through the motions. She was committed, in all the way, and her kids were loving it.

My own mother was never a young mother. She was forty-five when I was born, forty-six when my father lost his hands in that farming accident. I had no siblings. My mother, then, was the one to play catch with me, hit grounders and fly balls to me, throw passes with the football. Basketball I could play by myself. All I needed was a hoop and a ball. Baseball and football, though, were different matters. For those, I needed my mother, and she obliged.

I can't say whether it gave her much joy. She was a woman of duty, and perhaps she considered those athletic games with me chores she had to get done the same way she had to gather eggs, feed hogs, milk cows, help my father work on machinery, teach school, clean house, cook meals, do laundry. Or maybe she found some pleasure in the release from such responsibilities those times when she threw a baseball back and forth with me or tossed it up in the air and hit it with a bat or threw a football to me. Maybe our "games" took her away from her own cares.

I really don't know what to make of how my mother may or may not have felt about being pitcher, hitter, passer, nor can I say with any certainty why I'm worrying it around right now. Seeing that young mother playing roller hockey brought back all the memories of my mother and how, in her dresses and sensible shoes, she'd hit baseballs and toss wobbly spirals because there was no one else to do it.

If this has anything at all to do with writing, it's the fact that she taught me how to put aside fears and insecurities and to wade into territory that I might not believe myself suited for. Writing takes a measure of courage and a trust that you can make the journey simply because you must. Writing also takes a good bit of selfless love. My mother had that in abundance. She wasn't meant to pitch and hit and pass, but she did because I was her son and she loved me, and in the process she taught me how to love, how to give something of myself with no expectation of receiving anything in return. Each day, when I sit down at my writing desk, I practice what she taught me. I make a mark on a page. I set out on a journey. I don't know what to expect, so I expect nothing. I keep myself open to what might happen.

My Aunt among the Rocks

My Aunt Mildred will be having open heart surgery on Tuesday in Springfield, Illinois. I'll be there with her, remembering her stories of how when I was a small child, she would take me to the gravel road that ran by my grandmother's house and patiently sit with me while I hunted for rocks, which I found, for whatever reason, fascinating. I have no memory of this, but I feel it in every interaction between us—that patience, that encouragement, that love.

How fortunate I was to have the sort of aunt who would spend so many hours with a little boy who was intent on sorting through rocks. Patience and curiosity are essential to the development of a writer. We deal with those two qualities every day that we push words about the page. Although my aunt may not have known this, she was indulging my curiosity and teaching me that it was okay to take a good close look at things, to push the rocks around until I found some shape, some size, some texture, that interested me and made me decide it was a keeper.

It takes time and courage to look closely at something and to see the things that others have passed over. Isn't that what we do as writers? We poke and poke at situations, characters, images, language, until some precious thing emerges, precious because it's gone unnoticed by so many. We gather that thing up, that truth, and we shape it, and we carry it back to the other members of our human tribe. It's only ours to share, though, because we took the time to look, because we had the heart to care, because we had the need to know what we might find.

My aunt gave me those gifts. I've watched her put them to use in her own life: painting landscapes, tatting lace, quilting, growing glorious flowers, collecting antique music boxes. She taught me to look closely and not to be ashamed of having an artistic temperament. She taught me that it was not only all right but also necessary to search, to find, and to have the courage to say that something is beautiful or, if need be, to point out the ugliness that tries to keep us from seeing this glorious life.

Five Ways We Keep Ourselves from Writing

I was thinking recently of all the ways that we sometimes keep ourselves from writing. Here are but a few:

1. We wait for inspiration to strike. Sometimes, particularly in the early years of a writing career, we get the idea that our writing is the result of being inspired, and if we just don't feel inspired, well, then, we just don't, period, and we wait for that inspiration to come, and we wait, and we wait, and we wait. We need to recognize that when we write, we practice a craft, and the more we practice it, the better we become. It's not inspiration that we need; it's time, a quiet place, and effort.

2. We think we need to do more research. Research is seductive. We fall under its wiles, and the next thing we know, we aren't writing; we're reading. When I'm writing historical fiction or memoir, I tend to gather information and artifacts to the point that I see my characters moving through a very specific world and starting to talk to one another. Then it's time to write. I know that I'll go back later and fill in the gaps with more research, but once a story line launches itself in my mind, it's time to follow it. We can research the life out of something. We can know so much that there's nothing left to discover in the writing.

3. We think we have to be perfect. When you're writing a first draft, do you spend too much time writing and then rewriting a single sentence, a paragraph? If so, you're a sentence or a paragraph torturer. I've been one in my life. I know that desire to make everything perfect before moving on, but we *have* to move on.

Too much rewriting in a draft closes off spontaneous discovery. Produce pages; torture later.

4. We give into despair. We listen to the little voices in our heads, and those little voices tell us we'll never be good enough and that no one cares if we keep writing. That's true. No matter how much we succeed, we'll always think we can do better. If we stop writing, the world won't even notice. The world doesn't owe us that caring; we owe it to ourselves. So, accept the fact that our craft is one in which more often than not we feel as if we've fallen short. Don't give into despair. Use that feeling of wanting to be better to make yourself write more (see #1).

5. We're afraid to fail. Those little voices in our heads (damn, those little voices in our heads) tell us we're bound to fail. Tell those little voices to take note of what Samuel Beckett said: "Ever tried. Ever failed. No matter. Try again. Fail again. Fail better."

Here's what I know: we don't get anywhere by stopping. Whenever I used to tell my father I couldn't do something, he'd say, "Can't never did nothing." True enough. Writers have to write. We have to care enough to keep going. The little voices in our heads have a number of reasons why we shouldn't. Kill the little voices. Remember what former U.S. senator and professional basketball player Bill Bradley said: "When you are not practicing, remember, someone somewhere is practicing, and when you meet him he will win."

Five Things All Writers Can Control

Most writers are desperate for validation. We want someone to tell us we're good. We want to know we're good because people publish our work, talk about our work, give us awards for our work. We can spend a good deal of energy worrying about such things. The truth is so much of publishing and what happens beyond that is out of our hands. The time we spend worrying is time that could be better spent paying attention to the things we can actually control. So, here's my list, for whatever it's worth.

1. The amount of time we spend actually writing. It doesn't have to be a lot of time each day, but it should be consistent and uninterrupted. The more we write, the better we write. No one else cares a whit about how much time we're putting in, but we should care; we should care a great deal.

2. The amount of time we spend reading. I mean reading with an eye toward the artistic choices another writer makes and the effects those choices create. If we want to make something, we have to study how others have made it. We have to internalize their techniques.

3. The amount of time we spend engaging with the world. We writers can be loners. We're tempted to hole up in our private spaces and to stay there. But if we're not living, we're not really writing. I've always thought of my own work as a cycle of immersion and retreat, going out into the world and then coming back. As I age, I'm trying to expand my world by doing things and going places that are slightly out of my realm of experience. It gives me another lens through which to see the new as well as the familiar.

4. The degree of generosity that we have toward our fellow writers. Face it, what we do isn't easy, and yet we're sometimes loath to aid the development or applaud the success of others. Believe me when I say we're all part of the same club. Another's success benefits all of us (see #2). When we have a generous heart, we have an open heart. We take in more of the world, and our work becomes richer.

5. The way we handle disappointment. People will say no to you. No matter how much success you have, people will still say no to you. It's a fact, an occupational hazard. Get used to it. Toughen up. Use rejection to motivate you. Keep focused on the work (see #1). Keep writing.

Reading Like a Writer

One thing I always tell my students is that they have to learn to read the way a writer must if they're going to develop a deeper understanding of craft, but what does that really mean? How does a writer read?

I'll speak only for myself. Years ago I started reading with an eye for how a writer made a particular piece of writing. What artistic choices did he or she make to create particular effects? I'll restrict myself to prose, but I suspect the poets among you might be able to apply what I have to say to poetry. Writers should read not only to identify and eventually internalize specific artistic choices but also to further define their own aesthetics.

Openings

It's important to gauge our responses to the openings of pieces by thinking about the effects they have on us. Openings can come from different aesthetics and have different objectives, but the one thing they simply must have in common is they have to be interesting. We should think about the effects that different kinds of openings have and how the writer creates those effects. A good writer creates his or her ideal audience with the opening and also teaches that audience how to read.

Endings

The final moves of a piece are the ones that create the most resonance. Again, we should be able to articulate what the end of a particular piece makes us feel and to think about how the writer created that feeling inside us. What tricks of language, plot, thought, or image, among other things, did the writer use to give us a specific experience?

And Everything in the Middle

A piece of fiction or nonfiction often moves covertly to an ending that resonates with something we didn't anticipate. In fact, much of what a writer does involves raising certain expectations in the reader and then reversing them. I'm not only talking about misdirection of plot events here. I'm also talking about some quality of character or situation that's present from the beginning and that rises to the surface at the end. It's the pressures of plot—or sometimes in nonfiction it's the pressure of language, image, or thought rubbing together—that cause this latent energy to rise and to cause something to resonate within the reader once it does. Someone who is reading the way a writer reads will sweep back through the piece after feeling the impact of the ending and find everything in the middle that makes that ending possible.

Line by Line

Writers like moving words about on the page, paying attention to how syntax and structure create certain musical sounds. When we read as writers, we should highlight the sentences that make us laugh, make us weep, make us uncomfortable, make us feel at ease, and then think about how the writer created each of those effects merely through the arrangement of words in sentences. We should also think about how those sentences work together to create a particular mood or atmosphere.

What We Don't Like

We shouldn't be afraid to take note of passages that don't please us. Likewise, we should always be aware of pieces that are made up of satisfying parts but that don't add up to a satisfying whole. Pay attention to the sour notes. Think about how a writer got off the track. Think about what he or she might have done differently to create a more satisfying piece. Think of other artistic choices that might be more in service of what the piece intends. Start thinking the way writers do when writing, considering this move and then this move as they go through a trial and error process of determining the choices that will best allow the piece to resonate for their readers.

When we get in the habit of identifying choices and effects, we start to internalize moves that we can put to work in our own writing.

Writing to Preserve

I lost a pocket comb yesterday. It exists somewhere without me now. It was a black pocket comb, purchased in Anchorage, Alaska, to replace another comb that I lost there. I usually don't lose combs, but now I've lost two in two months.

Loss informs so much of my writing. I'm forever interested in what's been lost or what might be lost. Maybe it's because my father lost his hands when I was barely a year old. He became a different man, a man of temper, a sometimes violent man. While he was in the hospital, I stayed with my aunt and uncle. My aunt told me in her late years how she would take me to the waiting room at the hospital and my mother would come down to see me. I wouldn't let her hold me. I clung to my aunt. I suppose my entire world had been disrupted. I had a home, and then I didn't; I had a father with hands, and then suddenly I didn't. Loss is the legacy of my family. I come back to it again and again in my writing.

I wrote my first novel, *Quakertown*, because I was fascinated with a lost African American community in 1920s Texas. A renowned gardener, Henry Taylor, lived in that community before the city of Denton forced it to relocate to inferior land a few miles east of its location. I started my novel with the desire to figure out what it meant to call someplace home and to what lengths someone might go to preserve that place and the family that he was a part of there. I'd just moved to Texas, and I missed my native Midwest. I missed my connections to family members who had passed on, to those who remained, and to the places we'd always thought of as home.

The house where I grew up in the small Illinois town I'll always think of as home is vacant and in disrepair. Like so many of the homes that I remember from my boyhood, it's disappearing. Shrubs grow wild around its foundation; the grass is long and in need of mowing. Someone has taken a chainsaw to a fallen tree and left it in sections in the driveway. The garage is falling in on itself. The town itself is disappearing . . . at least the town as I recall it. My high school is gone. I was a member of the last graduating class before consolidation with the school in the next town over. The school building now houses an elementary school. The barbershop where I got my hair cut is gone, as is the sundries store where I bought candy and comic books and where my mother bought my first baseball glove, mistakenly buying a glove meant for a southpaw and thereby helping to make me ambidextrous. The nursing home where my grandmother lived the last years of her life is gone. The hardware stores where my father went for whatever he needed are gone. I can count at least five grocery stores that no longer exist, and the list goes on. I like to think of all those places and the people who passed through them.

Which leads me to this: writing is an act of preservation. No matter if we're creating fictional worlds, we're saving something, holding onto something, honoring something, even if that something is roughed up and ugly and scarred, even if it's something we wish we'd never known. When we write, we invite some piece of life to return. We're not just telling stories—real or fictional—or working with language and image in poems. We create in order to contain something, so a reader can say: "Yes, yes. This is how it is, was, will be."

Travel and the Writer

Because my father was a farmer, we didn't travel much when I was a kid. The crops and the livestock needed constant attention. A farmer can't afford to wander. It was only after my father sold our stock that we started to take a few trips. We went to the Illinois State Fair in Springfield one summer, and my father surprised us by suggesting that we go on to Hannibal, Missouri, and once we were there, he said we might as well drive on over to St. Joseph to see my mother's brother. Outside of a train trip to Washington DC, it turned out to be the longest trip we ever took as a family. I came home with a genuine Stetson hat purchased in St. Joe and the newfound knowledge that not every place was as flat as the farmland of southeastern Illinois. For the first time I'd seen the Mississippi River and its bluffs. I'd gone through Mark Twain Cave. I'd eaten pie à la mode at 2:00 a.m. in a diner in Chillicothe, Missouri. I was eleven years old, and suddenly the world was full of wonders.

Now, forty-seven years later, I've returned from a trip to Alaska, where the scenery was stunning and the people were friendly. I had a wonderful time talking with a waiter who took note of my Ohio State T-shirt (it really is true that wherever you go, you can shout out, "O-H," and someone will answer, "I-O") and chose to strike up a conversation. By the end of our chat I'd learned that he'd been at a reading I participated in at the Homer, Alaska, Elks' Club, and that he spent his summers in Alaska and much of the rest of the year in Thailand because he's a bird fanatic. He told me he lived in a hut on the beach and could manage on twelve dollars a day. He also told me things more intimate than this, things I'll keep to myself out of respect for his privacy.

Who knows what I may have gained during this conversation and others on my trip that will someday pay off for me in my writing.

The point is that the world is broad and the more corners of it we explore, the more material we have at our disposal. Travel opens the writer's mind and heart. We not only see new things; we respond to what we see with a fresh perspective. We stand in someone else's shoes. We live in someone else's skin. How can this not be good for the writer as he or she continues to practice the art of empathy? We even see ourselves anew because we see ourselves as outsiders the way the natives see us, and when we return home, we see everything around us with fresh eyes. Our response to our world deepens because we've had the chance to leave and then come back. As tiring and challenging as travel can be these days (lost bags, missed connections, cramped seats), there's always something to be gained for our art and for our living as well. Travel provides a contrast for the people we are and the worlds we occupy. That contrast helps us better understand others, both the people around us and the characters that we create or represent in our writing.

Slowing Down

In 1990 I bought a La-Z-Boy rocker/recliner for my study and spent a number of years sitting in it, writing. I still own that chair, and when I want some time to ponder or to daydream while working on an essay, a story, a novel, that's where I go. There's something about the gentle rocking motion that soothes me, and if there's a window nearby with a view, then all the better.

I used to write exclusively with pen and legal pad, and there's still something about the motion of my hand moving across the page that forces me to slow down, to feel the rhythm of my sentences, to open up avenues I might not consider while typing on a computer. I write almost exclusively on a computer now, but when I'm first getting something started or when I'm stuck and need to work something through, I often go back to the pen and the pad.

There's something to be said for slowing down in both our writing and our living. Paying attention to the natural rhythms of a piece will allow it to emerge more organically. Sometimes I feel something forced into its final form, and I wonder how much of that is the result of fingers flying over a keyboard and words stretching out over a computer screen. Think about what happens when you write in longhand. Try it and see. For me the world I'm describing emerges in fuller detail. I'm going slow. I'm taking the time to look around and see what's there. I can easily pause and look out a window or close my eyes, and while rocking back and forth, I can invite the world of the piece into my view. I also hear the music of the language. Writing in longhand reminds me that each word matters and that each sentence has a specific purpose in the piece.

Taking the time to listen, to gather, and to contemplate will lead to richer connections with the worlds and characters we're inventing on the page as well as with the people around us in our real lives. There's a reason why homes used to have front porches and on those porches were rocking chairs, swings, gliders. That gentle motion of back and forth, that slowing down of time, that careful consideration of words: it all matters if we'll allow it.

I was on a panel once about balancing work, life, and writing, and as always when I'm on a panel (surely this doesn't just happen to me?), I heard myself saying things with a voice of certainty, when really I wasn't certain at all. This is the way it usually goes for me. My Libra scales, seeking balance, cause me to see too many sides to the same question. I'm more of a person who wonders about certain things, hoping that the uncertainty of wondering might lead to considerations otherwise not possible, but I almost always fall victim to that panel persona of the one who knows exactly what he's talking about. People in the audience are asking questions, after all, and we panel members are the ones who are supposed to know the answers.

The truth, though, is that sometimes I say something on a panel and later start to wonder exactly what I meant. I start to question whether I had any right to say what I did. I start to question, and I think audience members should do the same. They should interrogate the answers of the panelists, trying to see if those answers have any validity, knowing, of course, that any answer from a panel member might make perfect sense for one person in the audience and still be bad advice for someone else.

So, in the midst of a conversation about the importance of carving out blocks of time for writing and staying obsessed with a project so you can't help but bring it to completion, I found myself saying that sometimes life gives us opportunities to rest and for the writer that can be a good thing because time away from a project can allow it to evolve in ways that it might not if we're forcing ourselves to keep slogging along. Leaving the project alone for a while can give the unconscious parts of our minds a chance to do some work with the material in the same way that we work on our lives through our night dreams. The result, once we return to the writing, is usually something we're more deeply attached to, moving through it now the way the dreamer does, by instinct, rather than woodenly trying to understand something through the logical parts of our brains. Simply put, we sometimes feel the material more deeply because we give ourselves permission to forget it.

Lordy Magordy! What kind of an enabler am I, telling people it's okay not to write? The older I get, though, the slower I become with my writing projects. It's not that I've lost my passion for the craft; it's just that I'm more at ease with being patient, letting something steep, waiting longer for completion, hoping that the rests I take might in the end result create something thicker, more textured, more resonant. By the same token I understand the importance of rest to make my writing seem fresh to me. Words, words, words: a lifetime of words. How easy it is to start to rely on the same tricks. When I was a younger writer, I could feel like everything I wrote was something I was making anew. Now, in what I'll call my more mature years, I sometimes crave rest and silence. They help me see my material with new eyes.

A good writing day can be spent daydreaming in my chair with no words put on the page. I feel, then, the same way I feel when I wake from a dream in the morning, like I have one foot in my real life and one still in that dreamworld. That's how writing feels to me when it's going really well, a happy blend of the conscious and the unconscious. More and more I'm starting to see the importance of rest for keeping me in that place from which my freshest writing comes.

Do I still have books I want to write? Absolutely. To write them the way they deserve to be written, though, I'm willing to wait, to give them time to deepen.

Our Quiet Places

I remember the silence of public libraries before they became places where people talk in normal tones of voice or even chat on cell phones. In summer the only sound may have been the gentle whirr of an oscillating fan. In winter there may have been the hiss of a steam radiator. People spoke in whispers when they had to ask the librarian something. It was a quiet place, and in that way it was holy.

I remember the country church that my mother took me to when I was a boy. Sometimes it got so quiet that I could hear the whisk of the tissue-thin Bible pages as people searched for Scriptures. I could hear a woman's pocketbook clasp shut as she closed it, having retrieved a handkerchief. I could hear the cellophane wrappers of cough drops being undone and the sound the cardboard fans made as people waved them through the air.

I remember a cemetery deep in the country (I still like to go there) where sometimes the only sounds came from a bobwhite's two-note call or from a hickory nut dropping from a tree to land in the grass.

As an only child growing up in the country, I developed an appreciation for solitude and quiet. I walked into the woods and listened to the creek water trickling over sandstone and shale. I moved through prairie grass, lost in daydreams, startled only by the clacking of wings when a covey of quail took flight.

A quiet place is necessary for a writer; at least it is for this writer. I fear it's getting harder and harder to find those stretches of quietude that allow our imaginations to deepen. I seem to recall that John Updike said that much of his work began for him while sitting in church. I'll confess to my own daydreams and flights of fancy while in the midst of a service. "What art offers is space," Updike said, "a certain breathing room for the spirit."

It's the "breathing room" of the creative process that we have to protect, and that breathing room comes from our quiet places. I fear, though, that modern technology is making it difficult. We are expected to be "connected," and thus we become part of the noise.

So here's a simple assignment meant to reclaim our right to shut out the clatter around us:

1. Go to a quiet place.
2. Get comfortable with being alone.
3. Let your mind wander.
4. Let it go where it wants, but pay attention to where it goes.

What Fills Us

Recently I made a trip to the farm my family owned in south-eastern Illinois. Yes, I was trespassing, but I took nothing but memories and a few photos, so I hope the current owners will understand. One of the photos was of the cistern behind the farmhouse. I remember, as a child, lowering a sorghum pail down into the water by a rope tied around its bail. I would let the pail fill with water and pull it back to light and air. Emptying and filling up, again and again, in this place that now never leaves me—this place I still think of as home.

This memory has led me to consider what fills us as writers—what makes it impossible for us to turn away from the page. Perhaps it's the thing we don't understand, that something that won't leave us alone, that nettlesome thing that we don't quite know what to do with, so we start to find a shape for it with words. A friend told me once about a man who made his living cleaning up crime scenes. I couldn't get that man out of my head. What was the rest of his life like once he'd spent his days cleaning up after murders and suicides? I had to write a story called "The Least You Need to Know" to try to find out.

Or maybe it's longing—a yearning for all to be right in the world. We know we can't create that rightness, can only come near it and know it by its absence, but we can't stop trying to capture it on the page. A little girl went missing in a town near mine when I was sixteen. She pedaled her bicycle to the public library one evening, and she never came home. The search for her haunted me then and does to this day. I wrote a novel called *The Bright Forever* because I was obsessed with time and space and the way people move through it. I thought about how small motions—actions or inactions—affect what's going to happen. I wrote a novel to try to save that little girl, but of course, I couldn't.

Or maybe it's rage. Maybe we rail against injustice. My first novel, *Quakertown*, was based on the true story of the forced relocation of a thriving African American community in 1920s Texas. I wrote a novel to protest that injustice, but I also knew I'd have to look at it from all perspectives. I'd have to forestall any judgment of who was right and who was wrong. I'd have to see the heroic sides of the villains and the ugly sides of the victims.

We fill ourselves up because we pay attention to the world. Simple as that. We take in the confusion and contradiction, the transient beauty, the pain, the loss, the joy, and because we are the sorts who are sensitive to everything around us, we find a way to give it voice. If we empty ourselves, we wait, knowing we'll soon be full again. Sometimes we want to stop. Sometimes we want to live a less examined life. But we can't. We're writers. We embrace the world in all its glory and despair. We go to the well again and again and again.

The Books and the Boys of Summer

Summertime and the reading is easy. It's that time when I can read the books I never find time to get to during the school year. I can range far and wide, from Michael Chabon's *Wonder Boys* to Gillian Flynn's *Gone Girl* to a rereading of *The Great Gatsby* to Katherine Boo's *Behind the Beautiful Forevers* to Russell Banks's *Affliction* to Jane Leavy's biography of Sandy Koufax. I read the way I did when I was a boy—indiscriminately—snatching off the library shelves whatever book happens to catch my eye.

Combining the books of summer with the boys of summer, I just finished *New York Times* columnist Dan Barry's *Bottom of the 33rd: Hope, Redemption, and Baseball's Longest Game*. This is the story of a minor league baseball game between the Pawtucket Red Sox, the Triple-A team of the Boston Red Sox, and the Rochester Red Wings, the Triple-A team of the Baltimore Orioles, that began on the Saturday before Easter in 1981 and was finally suspended early Sunday morning with the score tied 2–2 after thirty-two innings played. The game was continued from that point two months later, requiring only eighteen minutes for a Pawtucket victory in the bottom of the thirty-third inning. Winner of the 2012 PEN/ESPN Award for Literary Sports Writing, this is a book about much, much more than baseball. A book about the nature of timelessness, about loyalty, passion, community, and the pursuit of a dream. I dare say there are even some lessons for writers contained therein.

Imagine the eighteen fans who stayed through all thirty-two innings that April night and morning in spite of cold temperatures and frigid winds; imagine the players (some of them, such as Wade Boggs and Cal Ripken Jr., bound for greatness; others, like Dave Koz, who will eventually drive in the winning run for Pawtucket but will be unable to make that final climb from Triple-A to the big leagues) relying on their baseball instincts to prolong a game that has turned into an absurdity that begs to have an end. Players who want to get out of the cold, who want to sleep. Hitters who don't want to be 0 for 13. Pitchers who don't want to be the one to give up the game-winning hit. A catcher who has worked twenty-two innings. Men who keep doing what they've trained themselves to do: to pitch, to hit, to catch, to run, to throw. Imagine how time seems to disappear, how the stillness settles over the nearly empty park so the sounds of the bat against the ball, the grunt of a pitcher as he gets a little extra oomph behind his fastball, the whop of a cleat on the first base bag, the smack of the ball against the leather of a mitt, are clearly heard. Imagine that this will go on forever, baseball reduced to its purest elements, much the way it is on the sandlot when you're a kid and you keep playing no matter the score and sometimes after the score has been forgotten. Baseball played for the love of playing.

Imagine all of this and then think about writing. Think of all the hours spent alone in your writing room, writing poems, stories, essays, memoirs, novels, plays, screenplays, or whatever your genre of preference might be. If you're like me, you've got a number of manuscripts that will never be published, things you had to write in order to write the ones that do finally appear in print. You've spent countless hours doing what you love to do, which is to move words about on a blank page. And if you're like me, there will be countless times when you'll doubt the worth of what you're doing. What does it matter if this piece gets written? Trust me, it matters. Ask those men who played those thirty-three innings. Even if that game didn't amount to a hill of beans in the larger scheme of things, it meant something to those who played it, all of them with dreams of making it to the big leagues. They could have walked away as the night turned into morning. Imagine a baseball diamond with no players. But they couldn't walk away. The game wouldn't let them. Their passion wouldn't let them. Their talents wouldn't let them.

Again, if you're like me, you're prone to whining when the work isn't going well. You get all out of sorts. You wail out of fear of rejection. You say, "If only . . ." You look for targets upon which you can cast blame. You long for more time, more calm, more inspiration, more something.

I think about those men who played those thirty-three innings, and I tell myself: "Suck it up, Cupcake, and get in the game. Do what you love with thanksgiving. Celebrate the hours. There's writing to be done."

A Writer Writes

A Lifelong Apprenticeship

Each year in July my thoughts turn to my father, and I'm swept back to 1982 and my last summer spent near him. Two weeks before I'm to leave for the MFA program at the University of Arkansas in Fayetteville, he has his second heart attack and dies on a hot day while mowing the yard. The last words I ever say to him, just a week prior, are "Don't work too hard." He won't, he assures me, and I know he's lying. He grew up during the Great Depression, and work was with him the rest of his life. The fierce determination to get the job done no matter what it took was his great gift to me.

At the time the hardest thing I've ever done is to leave my widowed mother behind and make the four hundred–plus–mile drive to Fayetteville. I almost don't go. I almost back out to be near my mother during her time of grief. Maybe I should have done just that. Maybe that's what a good son would have done, but a dream dies hard. I wanted to be a writer. I went to Fayetteville, and by so doing, I began to learn that a writer is often leaving someone behind. The truth of this has deepened as the years have gone on. How many times I've retreated from loved ones for the sake of time spent holed up in my writing room, paying attention to the comings and goings of characters in stories or novels or with representations of family members in essays and memoirs.

Those two years that I spent at Arkansas taught me many lessons. One of them came down on me with a ferocity that left me reeling: after my first workshop where my story was ripped apart, I realized I'd been ill prepared for this part of my journey; I didn't know much of anything about how to write or what it meant to call oneself a writer. Today I'm still learning how much I don't know; each draft I face has something new to teach me.

Writing is a lifelong apprenticeship. I guess you'd say I was at ground zero after that first workshop, admitting that I knew nothing. Not a bad place to be, as Joseph Brodsky points out when he says, "A zero is at once the perfect emptiness and the most complete sense of possibility." I was in a place those early days at Arkansas from where I could open myself to what my instructors and my fellow writers had to teach me. Another lesson imparted: never let your ego get in your way of honing your craft. Someone always knows more than we do. No matter how long you write and no matter how many successes you have, there's always something more that you can learn.

At Arkansas I learned to read the way a writer must, with an eye toward how a story or essay or poem is made, with an eye toward the artistic choices a writer makes and the effects those choices create. I learned to listen to criticism. I learned that my first obligation was to the work itself and not to my own ego or to thoughts of publication and acclaim. I wanted those things, yes, but I most assuredly wanted them too soon. Dreams of success? Sure I had them, and more often than not, they were frustrated. I collected my rejection slips. I felt inadequate. I halfheartedly celebrated the successes of others. It would take me a while to understand that I wasted too much energy on disappointment, fear, envy—energy that would have been much more wisely spent on learning my craft.

It's hard to take ourselves and our self-interests out of the creative process, nigh on impossible, but one thing I know is that we should stop wanting things for ourselves and instead start wanting things for the writing that we're doing. Our obligation shouldn't be to ourselves and what we might gain from our writing but, instead, to the work itself and what it will gain from our fully realizing the impulse that first brought us to the page. I gradually began to learn to tune out the voices of ego and to listen to the work itself. I learned that a good deal of a writer's life is spent at a snail's pace. Sitting, for example. I'm very good at sitting. Staring out windows. I'm good at that too. Daydreaming? I'm first-rate. I learned that a writer has to be patient. I learned the joy of steady work. I learned that writing is self-perpetuating. The more you do it, the more you do it, and the more you do it, the more you do it. I learned, as Billy Crystal's writing instructor character tells his student, Danny DeVito, in the movie *Throw Momma from the Train*, "A writer writes."

I'm not sure that writing can ever flourish if approached from a hobbyist point of view. To me writing isn't something that someone dabbles in. You're either all the way in or you're not. Does that mean you have to quit your day job, hole up in a garret, and spend every waking minute writing? Of course not. We all have to face the realities of our lives. We have bills to pay, stomachs to fill with food, families to support.

When I finished my MFA program, I spent three years teaching at a technical college in southeastern Ohio. I taught five sections, mostly Freshman Composition, each quarter, with twenty-five to thirty students in each section. That makes for a lot of student essays to read and respond to, a lot of student conferences, a lot of classes to prepare. Somehow I still found time to write. I wrote between classes if I could. I wrote at night. I wrote on weekends. But what I remember to be the most exciting writing time of all took place on the fifteen-mile drives to and from campus, that time when I heard my characters engage in dialogue in my head, when I imagined what they might do next. The point is I lived inside my stories on those drives, and that was writing too. In fact, it made it so much easier the next time when I actually put pen to paper because by then I was chomping at the bit to get down what I'd already worked through in my head. And when I read craft essays by other writers, in addition to their novels and stories and personal essays or pieces of memoir? Well, that was writing time well spent too.

How much time can you set aside during the course of your day for writing? Two hours, one hour, thirty minutes? You'll be surprised at how many pages stack up over a year even if you only have a half-hour to devote to your writing each day. The important thing is to dedicate yourself to the life of a writer, to make that a part of the way you see yourself in the world. "A writer writes." Exactly.

Defeating Writer's Block

So, a time comes, eventually, when the writing isn't going well. It happens to all of us. We stare at the computer screen or the page, and we don't have a clue. It's like words have become bricks we try to lift with our tongues, or maybe language, tired of our ineptitude, has packed up and moved in with other writers, the ones who right now may be happily typing away—clackety, clack, clack, clack—while we sit in silence. Maybe we're unable to get a piece started, or maybe the piece we've been working on is refusing to cooperate.

Norman Mailer said, "Writer's block is only a failure of the ego." So, let's shake things up and restore our confidence. Here are a few things you can try to get the words flowing again.

The Jack Webb School of Writing: Just the Facts

Try evoking a specific world (either the world of the piece you're working on or any world that comes to you by making a list of details). What is there to be seen, heard, tasted, smelled, touched? Don't worry about making sentences; just daydream on the page. Often the sensory details will start to make characters come alive. You might actually start to see them moving and speaking, and if you do, you might find yourself in the midst of a scene. Usually sensory details draw out an emotional response from us, and if they do, then imagine what they might mean to your characters. I wrote my novel *River of Heaven* by first imagining the sensory details of two men building a doghouse in the shape of an elaborate sailing ship. The things of the world matter. Play around with them and see where they might take you.

The Serena and Venus Williams School
of Writing: A Volley of Dialogue

Let two characters do nothing but talk. Do it fast. Bop, bop, bop. Back and forth. Don't try to plan the exchange, just let it roll. Disengaging the rational part of the mind might just free you. You might get more playful, more serious, more outrageous, more whatever. Play large. Exaggerate. No easy lobs here, only blistering shots, again and again. Rapid-fire dialogue might hit upon something that will make you say, "Hmmm, now I have to write about that." The pressure of the fast exchange might open some aspect of what you've been working on that you haven't considered, or if you're trying to start something new, it might lead you into material you wouldn't have found otherwise.

The Sidney Poitier School of Writing:
"They Call Me *Mister* Tibbs!"

So many writers tell me that titles are hard. Okay, then, why not get the title out of the way from the get-go. Brainstorm. Anything is fair game. Memorable things you've heard people say, clichés, adages, other titles, place names, anything that makes you say, "Hey, I'm going to use that as a title someday." If you're lucky, something on your list will start to suggest material. You can always change the title later if you want to; the important thing is to find something that gets you started. Not too long ago, I wrote two stories for which I had the titles before I had anything else. They happened to be titles like the ones common for still life paintings: "Drunk Girl in Stilettos" and "Cat on a Bad Couch." I found that having these titles first gave me the interesting challenge of writing stories to fit them. The titles gave me a canvas, so to speak, and the impetus to fill it.

Which brings me to some thoughts about using other art forms. Look at photographs, paintings, sculptures. Read poems. Listen to music. Let the work of someone else touch something within you. I often think of writing as just one part of a larger conversation among all sorts of artists. I truly believe that I first began to write because I read, saw, or heard something that moved me and caused me to want to respond. Do whatever it takes to keep the words flowing even if that means leaving your desk and getting out into the world. Go places you wouldn't ordinarily go. Do things you wouldn't ordinarily do (within reason, of course). Let the world in all its glorious forms touch you, and then, write, write, write!

Ten Thoughts on the Writing Life

More and more these days I'm convinced that how we approach our work has a crucial connection to the quantity and quality of the work we produce. Much of our writing lives are spent in solitude, both physically and mentally. We often hope for good results so desperately that we rush the process. Sometimes we're too afraid of failure and too afraid to occupy the uncomfortable places where our writing takes us. We have to respect the fact that we're imperfect and may fall short of what we imagine for a particular piece, but we also have to be courageous enough to keep doing the work, trusting in our talents. Sometimes we'll succeed, and we'll be tempted to believe that now we've made it and from here on everything will be smooth sailing. It won't be. We need to accept that.

Each blank page or screen—each new piece—carries with it its own set of challenges to meet. When we fall short, we'll be tempted to fall into despair. We have to resist that temptation. We have to keep going steadily about our work. Being regular with our writing routines is a good thing. Writing is a self-generating process. The more we do it, the better we do it. This means we sometimes have to remove ourselves from our loved ones. We have to close the door to our writing rooms and have that period of uninterrupted time to work. We should never forget, though, to get out of those writing rooms to explore the world. We have to experience life before we can shape it. Success will come, no matter how slowly or intermittently. Writing is a lifelong apprenticeship, full of peaks and valleys. Take time to celebrate the peaks; don't dwell too long in the valleys. Take pleasure in the work.

1. We have to be comfortable with solitude.
2. We have to exercise patience.
3. We have to be fearless.
4. We have to be afraid.
5. We have to resist making too much of our successes.
6. We have to resist making too much of our shortcomings.
7. We have to put in the time and the effort.
8. We sometimes have to be selfish with our time even if we end up disappointing those who matter most to us.
9. We have to open ourselves to the world and all its mysteries and contradictions and wonders.
10. We have to take time to celebrate our successes but not too much time; we have to get back to work.

Keep Facing the Blank Page

These late winter mornings I hear birdsong. I hear birdsong even though the temperatures have been in the single digits or below zero, even though a new snowstorm sweeps through every few days. The birds don't know how to doubt. The turning of the earth tells them that spring is closer each day.

It takes a similar faith to be a writer. We come to the page with an idea of what we'll put there. We hold faith that something of value will emerge. We're believers. Every one of us who works with words believes in the value of that work. We come back to the blank page time and time again because we're convinced that this time we'll get it right. This time we'll succeed. This time the words on the page will do what we intend them to do.

Here are a few thoughts about how to keep facing that blank page:

1. Accept the fact that you will fail. Rarely will the thing you write measure up to the ideal that you first conceive.
2. Never let ego get in your way, neither excess nor lack thereof.
3. Humble yourself to the process. Somewhere there's a writer more talented who is also failing every day.
4. Celebrate your talent. Out of all the people in the world, you've been given this gift. Don't waste it.
5. Assert your right to do what you do best. Believe in yourself.
6. Be patient. Writing is your craft, and it takes practice. It requires a lifelong apprenticeship.
7. Be protective of your time. In large the world won't understand when you retreat to your writing room. Trust

that there are those of us who do. Trust that you belong to this community of writers.

8. Be willing to work. I'll repeat the quote from Bill Bradley: "When you are not practicing, remember, someone somewhere is practicing, and when you meet him he will win."

9. If you're going to whine or wallow in self-pity, make short work of it because it's all wasted energy. It's energy that could be better directed to your craft.

10. I'll remind you of what Samuel Beckett said: "Ever tried. Ever failed. No matter. Try Again. Fail again. Fail better."

What else are we to do, my friends, but the work that sustains us. Push on with hope, with faith, with the appreciation of what we love and how blessed we are to be able to face the blank page again and again each day, even this one, so close to spring.